Berlitz®
China

Text by Ken Bernstein
Updated by Dinah Gardner and J.D. Brown
Edited by Jeffery Pike
Cover photograph: Jeff Hunter/Getty Images
Series Editor: Tony Halliday

D0033175

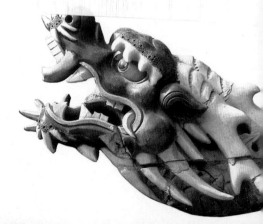

Berlitz POCKET GUIDE

China

Sixth Edition (2003)
Updated 2006
Reprinted 2006

PHOTOGRAPHY CREDITS
All photographs are by Nicholas Sumner, J.D. Brown or Bill Wassman except those on pages: 3 (middle)/UPPA Ltd; 6, 68, 99, 100, 199/Trip (W. Jacobs, A. Tovy, K. MacLaren, T. Bognar); 30, 32, 70, 74, 91, 118, 121, 122, 128, 142, 191/Topham Picturepoint; 19, 67, 73, 108, 186, 189/China Tourist Office; 78, 83, 129, 140, 172/Beifan.com; 26, 43, 46, 54/B. Handelman; 1, 23, 25, 50, 61, 63, 66, 77, 81, 169, 204, 210, 212, 220/Apa; 14–15, 82, 135, 139, 193, 195, 200, 201/ImagineChina; 16, 145, 150, 152, 162/Shen Kai; 92/E. Pansegrau; 109/Tony Halliday; 106, 126/Topham Imageworks; 113/Corbis; 137/Bodo Bondzio; 203/Manfred Morgenstern; 117, 124/Photobank Singapore; 95, 178/Panos (M. Henley, C. Towers); 156/ Topham PA; 208/Richard Nowitz; 215/Topham Star Images; 216/ Image Bank.

CONTACTING THE EDITORS
Every effort has been made to provide accurate information in this publication, but changes are inevitable. The publisher cannot be responsible for any resulting loss, inconvenience or injury. We would appreciate it if readers would call our attention to any errors or outdated information by contacting Berlitz Publishing, PO Box 7910, London SE1 1WE, UK. Fax: (44) 20 7403 0290; email: berlitz@apaguide.co.uk; www.berlitzpublishing.com

© 2006 Apa Publications GmbH & Co. Verlag KG, Singapore Branch, Singapore.

Printed in Singapore by Insight Print Services (Pte) Ltd, 38 Joo Koon Road, Singapore 628990.
Tel: (65) 6865-1600. Fax: (65) 6861-6438

Berlitz Trademark Reg. U.S. Patent Office and other countries. Marca Registrada. Used under licence from the Berlitz Investment Corporation

The Great Wall of China (page 64) winds from the Yellow Sea to the Gobi Desert

Take a boat trip along the Li River, flanked by exotic limestone spires (page 107)

The Forbidden City (page 53) was the Imperial Palace of the Ming dynasty

TOP TEN ATTRACTIONS

The Old Town of Lijiang, near Dali (page 86), is a UNESCO World Heritage Site

A cruise on the mighty Yangzi from Chongqing (page 81), through the magnificent Three Gorges

Suzhou, 'the Venice of the East' (page 159) is famous for its canals and its classical Chinese gardens

Shaolin Monastery, the birthplace of all the martial arts (page 156)

The army of terracotta warriors near Xi'an (page 188)

The statues in the Dazu Caves (page 83) include an enormous reclining Buddha

Sprawling Shanghai (page 144) is China's most forward-looking and dynamic city

CONTENTS

CHINA AND ITS PEOPLE

Ancient, vast, evolving and exciting, China is the trip of a lifetime. Its beauties – both natural and man-made – vie for attention: mist-muffled hills silhouetted behind sampans on a winding river; proud pavilions of brilliant red and gold; the Great Wall undulating over ridges and mountains receding far into the distance; an elegant vase of eggshell-thin porcelain that has survived the centuries.

Here, all the senses are engaged. Touch a 2,000-year-old inscription in stone or a bolt of newly woven silk. Taste the food of emperors. Listen to children singing. Smell the temple incense or a fresh melon in the marketplace.

English is the most widely spoken foreign language in China. Millions of Chinese study English in college or school (starting at the age of six), and through television programmes.

Getting to China means crossing more than mere oceans and time zones. It's another world, culturally, linguistically and ideologically. Real disorientation sets in with a blur of tenses, present and past. Ten minutes away from a modern hotel, water buffalo toil in the rice fields. To deliver half a ton of cabbage to market, a farmer and his son, harnessed, pull a primitive wagon. In a modern factory, artists copy thousand-year-old landscapes to sell to tourists paying with credit cards.

The world's oldest living civilisation can afford to be detached about time. It hasn't been long, in the overall scheme of things, since the Chinese gave the world gunpowder and the compass, paper and printing, porcelain and silk. And the works of the philosopher Confucius (551–479BC), the target of a book-burning binge in the 3rd century BC, were again wildly controversial in the 1970s.

A typical pavilion with upturned roofs, in Changsha, Hunan Province

The most obvious source of dislocation for the newly arrived traveller is the language. More people can read Chinese than any other language on earth, but the visitor, bewildered by the elegant characters, finds this no consolation. Spoken Chinese is tonal, making it supremely difficult for Westerners to master. But a few phrases under the belt will go a long way to earning you appreciation from locals.

Compounding the linguistic complications, the Chinese themselves speak a profusion of regional dialects – more than 150, some of them almost separate languages. Someone from the north can scarcely understand a word of the Cantonese spoken in the south. To help everyone communicate, the government encourages the use of an official spoken language, Putonghua (often known abroad as 'Mandarin'), based on the Beijing dialect. Happily, no matter what dialect a Chinese person uses in speech, the written language is universal. In addition, there are China's ethnic minorities, making up about 6 percent of the population, who speak tongues as diverse as Mongolian and Miao, Thai and Tibetan. In parts of the sparsely settled western deserts and mountains, the minorities are the majority.

> **You should feel free to discuss politics, religion or social problems with Chinese people, but refrain from argument or disrespect towards the country or its leaders.**

Language aside, the visitor's disorientation is further intensified by the timeless 'Chineseness' and the modern overlay of communism. Is the proliferation of polite but immovable bureaucrats a Marxist or a mandarin touch? Do families live three generations to an apartment because of tradition or because of the housing shortage? Why do Chinese infants almost never cry? Do they feel thoroughly loved or are they conditioned to be docile?

Every fourth child born into the world is Chinese. The well-known statistics come to life when you actually set foot in the most populous of all countries. China (including Taiwan) has almost 100 cities of more than one million inhabitants, and in any of them the rush-hour is as hair-raising as a traffic jam in New York or London. In the most crowded of all the provinces, Sichuan (Szechuan), you can journey for hours and never lose sight of people or houses, even in the most remote rural areas.

As you travel the country by rail or air, you cannot fail to be impressed by the work-intensive (that is, *human* work-intensive) agriculture. In the paddy fields you'll see hundreds of barefoot men and women collecting rice for processing by means of a single, hand-operated threshing machine. Farmers work every inch of ground that isn't rock or sand or nearly vertical.

The population includes more than 300 million children and teenagers

When you subtract the mountains, deserts and other totally inhospitable terrain, only a small fraction – around 10 percent – of China's great landmass is under cultivation, and problems are exacerbated by frequent floods and drought.

Geography and Climate

China is the world's third largest country by area, covering nearly 9.6 million sq km (3.7 million sq miles). Only Russia and Canada are larger. China is bordered (clockwise from the north) by Mongolia, Russia, North Korea, Vietnam, Laos, Burma, India, Bhutan, Nepal, India, Pakistan, Afghanistan, Tajikistan, Kyrgyzstan and Kazakhstan.

As you might expect over such a huge area, the weather blows hot and cold. It's about 5,800km (more than 3,600 miles) from northernmost China to the southern extremity, so while northerners are shovelling snow, southerners are sowing rice. Most of the rain falls in summer, mostly in southern and central China.

The most mountainous part of the country is the west, where the forbidding Himalayas reach their apogee with Mt Everest (8,850m/29,035ft), on the China-Nepal border. On the Chinese side, Everest is known as 'Qomolangma'. It is also in the west that the desert descends to about 150m (nearly 500ft) below sea level, so there's a vast topographic range. China's great rivers – the Yangzi, the Yellow and several other less legendary ones – rise in the west, and their waters are put to effective use in irrigation and hydroelectricity projects. The rivers also electrify Chinese life with the periodic drama of their floods, some of which have figured among mankind's great natural disasters.

Teeming Cities

Since the end of World War II, China's population has doubled to more than 1.3 billion. It is by far the most populous nation on earth, containing more than one-fifth of all the world's people.

Baby Rationing

Chinese toddlers are among the cutest in the world, but the stork brings only one baby to each family – and that's official policy. Chinese parents with only one child receive various benefits. If a second child is born, the privileges are revoked and social pressures applied. The government begins assessing penalties if the number of children rises to three. These restrictions – aimed at lowering China's alarming population growth rate – are applied with more flexibility in rural areas, where farmers tend to look upon children as producers of wealth: the more the better. The state's 'baby rationing' measures fly in the face of many Chinese traditions. The social repercussions (infanticide being only one) are just beginning to be appreciated.

There are 56 ethnic groups in China, of which the Han are by far the largest. Religious beliefs include Buddhism, Daoism, Confucianism, Islam and (for a very small minority) Christianity.

The bulk of China's vast population is concentrated in the country's east and south, where even a provincial town might have hundreds of thousands of inhabitants. Combining the world's most severe family-planning measures with restrictions on internal migration, the authorities have been trying to maintain the present balance of urban and rural populations by keeping the great majority in the countryside (around 65 percent). But

Early-morning _taiqiquan_ (t'ai chi) in a Shanghai park

despite these efforts, millions of surplus farm labourers pour into the cities in search of work. As a result, the big cities are immense: Shanghai, with 17 million residents, could well be the world's biggest. Beijing has a population of around 12 million, and Chongqing, Tianjin, Chengdu and Harbin nearly as many.

Riding a bicycle to work across any of these cities can be a daily chore taking one or two hours. The number of cars in China's cities has exploded since the turn of the century, making cycling more hazardous. It has also deepened the pollution problem caused by exhaust fumes spewed out from heavy trucks and buses.

The prospect of a long trek to the factory is only one of the disadvantages of big-city life. The housing is cramped and usually drab; shopping can be time-consuming and inconvenient.

But life in town is generally much more comfortable than in the countryside, and better facilities are available, from hospitals to schools. It's little wonder that many an ambitious villager dreams of the good life in urban society. But the government won't let him move to the city without a job.

The average wage is only about 1,000 yuan per month – the cost of an unexceptional dinner for four in a Beijing tourist hotel. If the salary level seems disastrously inadequate, remember that the cost of living in China is a small fraction of what it is in the West. Rent might run to only 100 yuan per month in rural areas, and basic foods are cheap. There are also mushrooming numbers of highly-paid individuals in the large cities who can afford cars, houses and all the luxuries of modern life.

Until recent years, the 'iron ricebowl' concept of assured income regardless of productivity was as firm a tradition as the daily siesta. For hundreds of millions of peasants, poverty was shared equally. Then, to the consternation of hard-line communist

A symbol of modern China: Shanghai's Nanpu bridge, opened in 1991

theoreticians, the post-Mao leadership decided to reward extra effort and good ideas with old-fashioned money.

Exploiting the Land

Only about 10 percent of China's land is cultivated. The soil is often unproductive, the climate is capricious, and the enormous population is constantly increasing. A drought or typhoon can still upset the balance between the supply of food and the demand, however modest each individual's requirements.

Every available scrap of usable land, including plots that seem impossibly arid or inaccessible, has to be exploited to the very limit, regardless of the scarcity of tractors, trucks, pumps and pipes. The problem is certainly not new, but the solutions adopted are. When the communists came to power in 1949, 10 percent of the population owned 70 percent of the land. The ideological breakthrough began on the farm, where reformers took aim at decades of lacklustre production; high costs, low yields and mismanagement had made farming uneconomical.

Realising that the people and the land were the country's most vital assets, the new regime set out to reorganise agriculture along more profitable lines. While allowing peasant smallholders to retain their property, the authorities confiscated land from wealthy landlords and redistributed the bulk of it to the previously landless masses. Slowly a new agricultural order evolved.

The Great Leap Forward

To begin with, mutual aid teams were formed in which labour, draught animals and implements were pooled. The next step was the development of cooperatives, in which land, animals and tools were held in common and income was shared. Sometimes as many as 200 families from one or more villages would join forces. Revenue would be collectively owned and invested for the welfare of all.

Mao Zedong believed that China could be industrialised rapidly, fuelled by idealogical motivation and the reorganisation of production. Not only the cities but also rural communities were encouraged to use their surplus labour and resources for heavy industries, especially steel production. Cooperatives were merged into an even larger unit – the commune – a group of villages and outlying hamlets responsible for local agricultural and industrial enterprises, commerce, education and home defence. By the end of 1958, virtually every peasant family was part of a people's commune.

'Backyard furnaces' were built to produce steel, but because of a lack of expertise, most of the steel produced was unusable. Agricultural production was expected to increase, and so local leaders falsely reported astronomical growth to advance their careers and avoid being called politically uncommitted. Between 1959 and 1961, the failure of the Great Leap Forward policies, combined with three years of bad weather, led to the 20th century's greatest famine.

The 'Second Revolution'

After the death of Mao Zedong in 1976, a gradual rehabilitation of individual initiative and the profit motive spread across the countryside. Farmers were first allowed, then encouraged, to devote themselves to their private plots. Incentives were phased in so that peasants were allowed to sell their surplus production and the yield of their private gardens for whatever the market would bear.

Mechanisation has been slow to make an impact on rural life

With a green light for cottage industries, rural profits snow-balled. The new approach to agriculture soon filled the markets with an abundance of produce and improved the living standards of enterprising farmers.

The success of the new agricultural policy was so striking that the authorities turned to the industrial field. To the dismay of traditional ideologues, Beijing called for a decentralised economy. Factory managers were instructed to adapt to market pressures, although the method of doing so often defied solution. At the same time, private entrepreneurs were allowed to open their own restaurants, shops and service industries. The infallibility of Marx and Lenin was officially questioned: the

Throughout China, the bicycle is still the ubiquitous beast of burden

People's Daily conceded that the prophets of communism could not solve all modern-day problems.

Life on the Farm

If you have a chance to visit a rural community, don't miss it. After all, it's the life of 65 percent of China's population. From all you've heard about communes, you might imagine barracks for living quarters and a mess hall for dinner. Instead you'll find a collection of villages, each a cluster of single-storey brick or cement-block houses or, in poorer regions, a scattering of mud huts with thatched roofs. In the main street of each village (which probably isn't paved) a shop sells everything from cotton rations to pots and pans. Bicycle repairmen hammer and clang, old men play cards and apple-cheeked children peer curiously at foreigners. In richer villages, it's a different story. You'll find houses that resemble modern villas. Inside, the amenities can rival those of China's most prosperous cities, from TVs to microwaves, and perhaps even a computer.

Many of China's most prosperous farmers are concentrating less on farming than on sideline industries. Hancunhe, one of 11 villages in a commune near Beijing, illustrates this trend. Destitute in 1978, the village formed a construction company of local bricklayers to build homes and offices for Beijing's rising middle class. By the mid-1990s, the village had 6,000 employees working in construction and the company's income had surpassed US$7 million annually. As for farming, this village recently invested over US$2 million in greenhouses from California to grow organic vegetables, all the rage in up-market eateries in Beijing. These villagers still farm, but with paved streets and new homes, their village looks like a modern suburb.

Life on many farms, of course, continues to be harsh, with back-breaking work and long hours. Increased mechanisation is beginning to ease the peasants' burden in more remote areas. With bureaucratic constraints relaxed and grassroots initiative rewarded, peasants with imagination and energy are earning money – sometimes small fortunes – in the free markets of nearby villages and towns, selling surplus produce and the yield of their private plots and whatever they can manufacture. The official policy now smiles on enthusiastic peasants who 'get rich first', because unless those in the countryside prosper, those in the cities can hardly rest easy.

Tourist Excursions

For the tourist, the utter strangeness of the organisation of agriculture and industry adds much to the fascination of China, and tourism authorities routinely arrange excursions to factories and farms. Originally a propaganda exercise, these tours proved a great success. There is no longer any attempt to deny evident shortcomings. Nor do official guides disguise the fact that they are showing off model institutions of which the nation is proud, and not necessarily typical establishments. If your tour group happens to be served a nine-course banquet at a collective farm's canteen, no one will try to convince you that this is the way ordinary farmers really live.

Such excursions are among the advantages of package tours to China. You might not know in advance (even one day in advance) what's on the agenda, although the local tourism authorities try hard to organise varied and fulfilling programmes. There is no objection to foregoing any of these outings, but you should tell your guide in advance so the rest of the group doesn't waste time waiting for you.

Independent travel is a recent innovation in this country that is barely accustomed to the idea of group tourism; after all, tourists of any kind were almost unknown in China until the late 1970s. Facilities are still so limited that spur-of-the-moment travel is a very chancy affair. But if you want to compose your own itinerary, and you don't mind queuing up and trying to explain your problems at railway stations, airports and hotel reception desks, the adventure can be appealing.

China's formal tourist attractions are so varied and so widely dispersed that a first trip can be little more than a preview. Even

The Art of Lacquer

Since the feudal Zhou dynasty, some 2,500 years ago, works of art in lacquer, a resinous varnish, have been a Chinese speciality. The lacquer and the dyes used are of a particular type, and applying the various layers of this fragile material is a time-consuming exercise. Sometimes, as in the Song style, layers of different colours are applied, each highly polished, then the finished object is engraved to reveal its multiple nuances. In the sumptuous Tang pieces, the shimmering surface is painted or inlaid with mother-of-pearl.

Lacquer is used to decorate boxes, fans, plates, musical instruments, furniture, and the pillars of temples and palaces. Examples from the Ming and Qing dynasties, delicately engraved and painted in red, are still copied today.

Many Chinese towns and villages have at least one lacquer factory where tourists can watch the manufacturing process, which is still largely carried out by hand.

if time and money permit one of those grand tours of more than three weeks, you will probably have to choose between a Yangtze River voyage and the Mogao Grottoes, or between the Stone Forest and the Silk Road. Whatever your itinerary, you are sure to experience the incredible diversity of China: the sweeping roofs of a historic temple in the morning, a classic mountain panorama in the afternoon and acrobatic performances or folk music in the evening. Somehow everyone manages to squeeze in three meals and some shopping as well.

The well-named Catch-Cloud Pavilion on Piled-Silk Hill, Guilin

Eating and Shopping

Most tourists would agree that the food in China rates as an attraction in itself. Whether you're attending an official banquet or trying your luck at a noodle stall, there's really nothing like it anywhere else in the world. Now is the time to sample all the classic recipes prepared with genuine ingredients in the time-honoured manner. *(See the Eating Out chapter, on page 218, for more detailed recommendations.)*

Souvenir shopping is on almost every visitor's must-do list. Tourist areas are always packed with stalls and markets selling all manner of goods from faux antiques to the real thing. Typically on offer are ceramics, jade, silk, paintings, traditional clothes and a wealth of other mementoes.

As well as the tourist markets, you can find heaps of bargains in neighbourhood department stores. Shopping malls in larger cities, such as Beijing and Shanghai, are packed with genuine

Western-branded goods as well as the pirated versions. You will also find some familiar names like Carrefour and Wal-Mart. In smaller towns or remote areas where minorities live you may find local products unique to that area.

Exotic Entertainment

After a long, hard day, you might be tempted to miss the 'nightlife' proposed on the timetable. All the same, summon up your strength and accept an invitation to the local cultural palace or theatre. This could be your only chance to see an authentic Peking opera (or Cantonese opera or Szechuan opera, which are quite different), or acrobats daring the world from dizzying heights, or comics you will laugh at without understanding a single word they say. Whatever the programme, it's bound to be full of insights into the latest cultural directives. The unadvertised stars of the show usually are the audience itself. They tend to be miserly with the applause, but don't let that inhibit you.

Even after you've seen the historical and artistic treasures, the cities and the breathtaking countryside, you can still find reasons to keep coming back to China. Some visitors take courses in acupuncture, for instance, or study Chinese martial arts or Chinese opera from a backstage perspective. There are culinary package tours, as well; presumably the survivors can rustle up Peking duck in their own kitchens.

The most unforgettable experience of China is being among the people. Just walk out of your hotel early in the morning and wade into the sea of China's billion people: there are waves of jingling bicycles, anxious throngs at bus stops, and neighbours doing slow-motion callisthenics with pauses for gossip. Holding a bird cage up high, a pensioner takes his canary out for an airing. At a busy corner stall, Chinese snacks are prepared, sold and consumed.

The way these people dress, work and relax never fails to fascinate the foreigner. Of course, the curiosity is more than reciprocated. You might sometimes feel uncomfortable, so avid is the attention you attract. But you couldn't want a friendlier welcome.

Notes about Spelling

For the past century, the commonest way to spell Chinese words in roman letters was the Wade-Giles method. Increasingly, however, *pinyin* (literally 'phonetic sound') is the modern standard, and is the official system used inside the People's Republic. (Taiwan, on the other hand, still uses the Wade-Giles system.)

This book uses *pinyin*. Travellers will encounter both forms of spelling in Asia, so must sometimes make certain linguistic leaps of recognition. The capital was spelt Peking in the Wade-Giles method, and is now Beijing in *pinyin*. The founder of the Communist party used to be Mao Tse-tung; now he's Mao Zedong. The goddess of mercy is still Kuan Yin in Taiwan, but is Guanyin in *pinyin* China.

The only *pinyin* transliterations that are not fairly obvious as regards pronunciation are *qi*, which is pronounced *chee*, and *xi*, pronounced *shee*. Thus, the Ch'in dynasty is now the Qin dynasty, and the ancient capital Sian is now Xi'an.

A Chinese Chess game attracts spectators in Tiantan Park, Beijing

A BRIEF HISTORY

Hundreds of thousands of years before China was to become the world's longest-running civilisation, the prologue was enacted by means of the flicker of a carefully tended fire. 'Peking Man' – a species known as *Homo erectus*, a forebear of *Homo sapiens* – achieved a mastery of fire. We might call it the first Chinese invention. Not that he devised any way of *creating* fire. Peking Man simply learnt how to capture flame, perhaps from a forest fire, and keep it alight. He thus enjoyed two revolutionary luxuries: light and heat.

> From as early as the neolithic period, the Chinese made silk from thread produced by the caterpillars they cultivated on the leaves of mulberry trees.
> It remained a closely guarded Chinese secret until the 6th century AD, when silkworms were smuggled to the West.

Technologically and sociologically, it was a phenomenal breakthrough: with fire, communities could live year-round in one cave, in which cooking and even smelting could be pursued. And so, by 600,000BC, about 50km (31 miles) southwest of present-day Beijing, the ancestors of mankind were ready to settle down. Several hundred thousand years later, when Marco Polo reached the capital of China, he was astonished by a further development in fire technology. The Chinese, he announced, used black stones dug out of mountains as fuel. Europeans did not yet have a word for 'coal', nor had they discovered a use for it.

The First Dynasties

The confluence of mythology and history in China took place around 4,000 years ago during what is referred to as the Xia (Hsia) dynasty. This was still the Stone Age, but the people are thought to have mastered the art of making silk *(see box, above)*, and written language was already in use, originally by oracles and then by official scribes – China's first scholars.

During the second of the quasi-legendary dynasties, the Shang (from about the 16th to 11th centuries BC), the Chinese developed an interest in art. Careful geometric designs as well as dragon and bird motifs adorned bowls and implements. And with the arrival of the Bronze Age, the Chinese created bronze vessels of such beauty and originality that, until recently, Western archaeologists refused to believe they were cast 3,000 years ago.

The Shang gave rise to the concept of one Chinese nation under one government. Among the advances of the era were the introduction of astronomical calculations, the use of cowrie shells as a unit of exchange, the construction of palaces and temples, and the refinement of table manners through the introduction of chopsticks.

The Zhou (Chou) clan had long been vassals of the Shang, but eventually grew strong enough to defeat them in warfare in the 11th century. They continued to hold sway until the 5th century BC. They built a capital at Chang'an (now called Xi'an) and the sons

Chinese writing has an unbroken history of more than 4,000 years

of Zhou rulers were dispatched to preside over vassal states in a feudal-like system. Chinese boundaries were expanded, land reform was instituted and towns were built. But perhaps more significantly, the declining years of the Zhou era produced two of China's most influential thinkers.

In the rest of the world, China's supreme sage, Kongfuzi (K'ung Fu-tzu), is better known by the romanised name 'Confucius'. He was born in 551BC in what is now Shandong Province in eastern China. So profound was his influence that 11 Chinese emperors made pilgrimages to the birthplace of the Great Teacher. You, too, can pay your respects at the vast temple raised on the site of his home in the small town of Qufu, and at his tomb in the woods just to the north.

The classics of Confucius, while seldom addressing spiritual and metaphysical matters, set standards for social and political conduct that still underlie many of the Chinese ways of doing and perceiving. Confucius laid great stress on the proper and harmonious relationships between ruler and subject, parent and child, teacher and student, the individual and the state. These relationships were deemed to be hierarchical and dictatorial. If the order was disturbed, dire consequences inevitably resulted. The son who disobeyed the father would bring disaster upon himself and his family, just as the emperor who defied the 'mandate of heaven' or ignored the good of the empire brought ruin upon the nation.

Chinese craftsmen of the Shang dynasty mastered the art of bronze casting. First a wax model was coated with clay and fired. This melted the wax and hardened the clay into a mould, into which molten bronze was poured. More elaborate Shang bronzes were moulded in several sections then assembled.

Over the centuries Confucius has suffered more changes of fortune than probably any other philosopher. Honoured soon after his death as the greatest of scholars, he was later revered as semi-divine; you can still visit temples to Confucius in many cities. But during the Cultural Revolution (1966–76) he was denounced as a counter-revolutionary force. It was only after the death of Chairman Mao (1976) and the opening of China to the outside world under more progressive reformers that Confucius, too, was 'rehabilitated'.

Unlike Confucius, about whose life many specific and even colourful details are known, the philosopher Laozi (Lao Tse or Lao-Tzu) is something of an enigma. Estimates of his date of birth vary by well over a century. One legend even says he taught the young Confucius. Laozi is immortalised by his book of thoughts on man, nature and the universe, *Daodejing* ('The Way and Its Power'), which became the major text of China's greatest indigenous religion, Daoism (Taoism). With its emphasis on nature, intuition, the individual, paradox ('the knowledge which is not knowledge') and the cosmic flow known as 'the Way', Daoism became the religion of artists and philosophers.

Statue of Confucius in the Beijing temple dedicated to the sage

After the death of Confucius, the Zhou dynasty entered a period of strife known as the 'Warring States' period (475–221 BC). Despite political strife, social and economic advances included the introduction of iron, the development of infantry armies, the circulation of currency, the beginning of private land ownership, the expansion of cities and the breakdown of class barriers. Orthodox communist histories make this era the dividing line between a 'slave society' and a 'feudal society'. It would give birth to the first emperor to unify China.

The Chinese Empire

The word *China* is a relatively recent innovation, believed to be derived by foreigners from the name Qin (Ch'in), the first dynasty to unify China after the Warring States period. 'China', of course, is a non-Chinese term. Even today, the Chinese still call their nation *Zhongguo* (literally 'Middle Kingdom'), referring to its position at the centre of the universe in respect to heaven and earth.

Under the First Emperor, Qinshi Huangdi (221–206BC), the empire was organised along strict lines. Land was divided into provinces and prefectures, with power vested in a central government staffed by highly educated bureaucrats. Disapproved books were burned and dissidents were either executed or exiled. Canals, roads and the Great Wall were built under the auspices of an extensive public works programme staffed mostly by conscripts. Official decrees standardised weights and measures and even the axle dimensions of all wagons (the latter

The Great Wall was first linked together in the 3rd century BC

edict kept transport in the same ruts for countless years). You can visit a site of the Qin dynasty today at Xi'an, where the First Emperor's terracotta army was unearthed in 1974 *(see page 188)*.

The great Han dynasty (206BC–AD220), which followed the Qin, consolidated the imperialistic order. Civil servants were selected by exams, the centralised government standardised currency, and the 'Silk Road' across central Asia opened up global trade. On the military front, the Han triumphed over marauding Huns and the Central Asian nomads, and Chinese sovereignty was extended almost to today's frontiers. The development of a new crossbow – which was a longer-range and more accurate weapon than China's foes could deploy – ensured Han supremacy.

A golden age began, and a university was established in the capital city, Chang'an (now Xi'an). Intellectuals, who had been harried by the Qin, were now encouraged in their creative endeavours, and with the invention of paper, the influence of their writings became more widespread. Trade and industry developed and communication systems improved. Sculpture, ceramics and silk manufacture flourished. And the arrival of Buddhism, a new religion which came to China from India via Tibet, was to have an enduring effect on Chinese life and art.

The Three Kingdoms

Like many dynasties before and after, the Han succession ended around AD220 in a new struggle for power and anarchy. As a result, the nation was split into three competing kingdoms. The era of the Three Kingdoms lasted only about half a century, but it had as a legacy some thrilling tales of derring-do that later inspired various plays and a classic Ming dynasty novel. And the first mention of tea-drinking in China occurs in the 3rd century, a footnote of fascination for social historians.

Over the next several hundred years a series of dynasties, some led by foreign rulers, held power under almost constant threat from usurpers at home and abroad. Regionalism and class distinction re-emerged and strong national government was set back by division and conflict. During this period many people moved to the south and the Yangzi (Yangtze) valley became the leading centre of Chinese culture. As for foreign invaders, they brought new ideas but, as often happened in China, they were assimilated into the more advanced society of the Middle Kingdom.

National unity and strength were renewed under the Sui dynasty (AD581–618), a brief prelude to the highest achievements of Chinese art. The Sui built a stately new metropolis at Chang'an, near the site of the old Han capital (present-day Xi'an, in Shaanxi Province). They also began work on the Grand Canal, which was to link the rice-growing areas of the Yangzi valley with Beijing, an engineering achievement comparable to the construction of the Great Wall.

Buddhism in China

Founded in India in the 6th century BC, Buddhism is believed to have reached China about 500 years later. It was brought by merchants who arrived in caravans via the Silk Road, the trade routes that were later travelled by Marco Polo. Monumental artworks in the caves at Dunhuang, created in the 4th and 5th centuries AD, reveal that Buddhism had long been flourishing in western China. By the time of the Tang Dynasty, Buddhist temples and pagodas were a prominent feature of the Chinese landscape, and Buddhist monks, pilgrims and worshippers numbered in the hundreds of thousands. Several Tang emperors officially supported the religion; the empress Wu Zetian, in particular, surrounded herself with Buddhist advisers.

Buddhism reached its zenith in China in the 9th century, but it has continued to shape Chinese culture to the present day, especially in its Chan (Zen) school. The temples and sculptures that survive are among China's leading tourist attractions. Today about 70 million Chinese (about 6 percent of the population) are Buddhists, and the temples are active places of worship.

The Glory of the Tang

In the realm of culture, no era of Chinese history has surpassed the Tang (T'ang) dynasty (618–907), during which poetry and art reached a brilliant apex. China's Imperial Academy of Letters was founded, about 900 years before any such institution was established in Europe. The first known printed book, a Buddhist scripture, was published in China in 868.

The invention of paper brought a flowering of calligraphy

The capital city, Chang'an, had a population of more than a million, which was far more people than European cities had at the time. In Chang'an, extravagant palaces and temples were interspersed with markets stocked with exotica from as far away as Byzantium. Foreign traders journeyed here to purchase silk, porcelain and spices and, by so doing, introduced the Chinese to foreign ideas.

Scholars, poets and artists all achieved prominence. Encyclopaedias were compiled, and poetry evolved a metric system and lines that rhymed. As Buddhism gained strength and took on a Chinese character, it inspired the construction of great temples and pagodas adorned with frescoes and statues. Artists painted sensitive landscapes and perfected the subtle brushwork of calligraphy. Sculptors excelled in portraying lifelike human, animal and religious figures.

Yet by the beginning of the 10th century, the Tang rulers had lost their control of the country. Revenues from tax collection dwindled, ambitious palace eunuchs plotted, reform schemes failed and rebellious forces threatened. The emperors distributed their wealth and largess to too many warlords, hoping to

Sculpture from the Tang dynasty is both lifelike and lively

pacify them. By 907 the people could see, through all the turmoil and confusion, that the Tang dynasty had lost the 'mandate of heaven', and so it was that the last of the Tang monarchs abdicated.

The Song Bring Stability

Chinese historians designate the next half-century as the era of 'The Five Dynasties and the Ten Kingdoms'. This transitional period was marred by political and military infighting, and by rivalry, intrigue and cruelty. Then, an able general named Zhaokuangyin (Chao K'uang-yin) came onto the scene and founded the Song (Sung) dynasty (960–1280), which ensured Chinese cultural supremacy for the next three centuries.

The number of cities in China increased dramatically under the Song, mostly in the Yangzi valley and in the southeast. Where there were cities, there were scholars, artists and artisans. Moveable type revolutionised printing, books became more common and literacy increased; Chinese scientists published works on botany, astronomy, mathematics and geography.

Emperors appointed court painters, and glazed porcelain was received abroad with admiration and awe.

But while art and scholarship continued to thrive, the political and military situation deteriorated under the Song. Foreign invaders chipped away at the empire. Taxpayers groaned under the burden of the army and the tribute paid to foreign rivals, and complained about the luxuries of palace life. Disaster was inevitable: invaders from Manchuria forced the Song to retreat to the south. And the Mongol invaders, headed by Genghis Khan, swept across China, bringing the country under foreign rule for the first time.

Under Mongol Rule

A poignant drama signalled the Mongol conquest of China (1279–1368). After 20 years of resistance, the Song armies were finally ready to capitulate. The boy emperor was hidden aboard a ship, but when it was surrounded by enemy craft, the last of the loyal commanders seized the eight-year-old monarch in his arms and leapt with him to his death in the sea.

The new era, known as the Yuan dynasty, lasted less than a century. Creativity declined, but the new ruler of China, Kublai Khan (grandson of the great Genghis Khan), had an open mind and a generally humane attitude. He appointed Chinese bureaucrats and scholars to help rule the country. Historians generally conclude that Kublai Khan became an 'almost authentic' Chinese emperor, that the conquerors changed more profoundly than the conquered.

The capital of the new empire was built on the site of present-day Beijing and was called 'Dadu' or, in Mongolian, 'Cambaluc' – spelled Kanbalu by that most renowned of medieval travellers, Marco Polo. His account of the vast new capital throbs with admiration for the palaces and bazaars and the profusion of shade trees. He regards with wonder the Great Khan's religious tolerance, generosity and admirable taste in wives. He reports all manner of innovations, not least the invention of paper money. (Counterfeiting, he reports, had also been discovered.)

Marco Polo's account of life in legendary Cathay was received with incredulity in Europe, where it was suggested that his

The Mongol emperor Kublai Khan receives a gift of pearls

imagination had run wild. What else could Venetian citizens make of his report that the 'noble and magnificent city of Kin-sai' (now Hangzhou) had 12,000 bridges, many so high that sailing ships could pass under them?

With the death of Kublai Khan (in 1294, at the age of 80), the Mongols started to lose their grip. The great emperor's successors lacked his vision and vigour. Insurrection was in the air, met by oppression and resulting in ever more sustained resistance. Finally, a full-scale uprising led by a peasant general, Zhuyuanzhang (Chu Yüan-chang), routed the Yuan rulers. In 1368 Zhuyuanzhang assumed the throne of the Middle Kingdom, founding yet another dynasty – the Ming.

The Brilliance of Ming

In Chinese, the word Ming is written as a composite of the characters for 'sun' and 'moon', which are combined to mean 'brilliant' or 'glorious'. In fact, the dynasty (1368–1644) didn't quite live up to its name. Beauty was achieved in architecture, sculpture and the decorative arts. But literature, now serving an ever-wider audience, produced few masterworks, and philosophy saw no new developments. Science, which had been far more advanced than in Europe, was so gravely neglected that China became a technological backwater.

Perhaps to compensate for the Mongol interlude, the Ming emperors opted for traditional Chinese values. The keeper of the 'mandate of heaven' played his role to the autocratic hilt, while bureaucrats kept their jobs (and heads) by paying him lip service.

Conservatism and hostility to foreign ideas, however, could not be absolutely maintained. During the Ming era, China imported tobacco, pineapples, peanuts and syphilis. The first Christian missionaries came to China with the arrival at Guangzhou, in 1516, of Portuguese ships. Thanks to the emancipated Confucian tradition, they were usually welcomed, although they hardly achieved mass conversions. From the Jesuits the Chinese learnt mathematics and astronomy.

At first the Ming headquarters were moved south to the Yangzi River port of Nanjing ('Southern Capital'), but at the beginning of the 15th century the capital returned to what was now renamed Beijing ('Northern Capital'). Here Ming architects and artisans produced some of China's most elegant palaces, temples and parks, including the Forbidden City and Temple of Heaven, masterpieces that survive today.

A Galaxy of Firsts

Many inventions first saw the light in China, often centuries before they reached the West. The Chinese produced cast iron from the 4th century BC, 1,800 years before Europe discovered the technique. From the 1st century AD – 1,000 years before Europe – paper was made by pulping rags and wood fibre. Block printing was known in China in the 9th century, and movable type came into use a couple of hundred years later. Printing was not invented in Europe until 1440.

The Chinese made mechanical clocks, powered by a water-wheel, from the 8th century. Water was also used to drive early textile and winnowing machinery. They were the first to build suspension bridges, combining bamboo and cast-iron chains. They invented the foot-stirrup, which revolutionised cavalry warfare, and gunpowder, which was used to propel arrows from bamboo tubes – the first rockets.

The magnetic compass was another Chinese first, and at least 200 years before vaccination was developed in Europe, Chinese doctors were practising immunisation by placing pus from a smallpox pustule in a patient's nostril.

The move northwards made the supervision of defence efforts on the ever-sensitive borders of the empire easier. The Ming rulers oversaw the construction and renovation of the sections of the Great Wall that millions of tourists visit today, but even this eventually proved incapable of keeping out enemies. By the 17th century, after repeated forays, infiltrations and invasions, forces from Manchuria capitalised on domestic upheavals in China to take power in Beijing, almost by default. But consolidating control over the rest of the country was a long and brutal business. The Manchu invaders called their new dynasty the Qing (Ch'ing). It held power until modern times (1644–1911).

> In addition to their Christian texts, Jesuit missionaries published over 100 treatises in Chinese on Western science and technology. Outstanding among them was the Italian Matteo Ricci, who mastered Chinese, devised his own system of transliteration and compiled a dictionary.

Pigtails and Prosperity

The invading 'barbarians', the Manchu, adopted all the refinements of Chinese civilisation, installing a regime so conservative that it began to hold back progress. But for all their Confucian outlook and traditionalism, the Manchu imposed one singular feature of their own culture: the wearing of pigtails. Ironically, this was one peculiarity the rest of the world came to consider typically Chinese.

One of the most dynamic emperors was Kangxi (K'ang-hsi), who reigned at almost the same time as Louis XIV of France. He presided over an era of prosperity and positive achievement, rebuilding Beijing, encouraging scholarship and expanding the empire to its greatest area. By his predecessors' standards, Kangxi lived modestly; his concubines numbered no more than 300.

Under Emperor Qianlong (Ch'ien Lung), Kangxi's grandson, conflict arose between Europe's empires and the Middle Kingdom. King George III of Britain sent an emissary to negotiate diplomatic and trade relations. The emperor flatly turned him down but thanked him for showing such 'submissive loyalty in sending this tribute mission'. No insult appears to have been intended, even though the message referred to Britain as 'the lonely remoteness of your island, cut off from the world by intervening wastes of sea.' China sincerely believed itself to be the centre of the world: it had nothing to learn or gain from so-called foreign devils. But such sublime self-assurance was to be short-lived.

The soaring demand in Europe for Chinese tea, silk and porcelain brought increasing pressure for freer trade. However, the Chinese were stubborn. Needing no commodities, they would accept only silver bullion in exchange for goods, thus undermining Britain's balance of payments. Then, at about the turn of the 19th century, wily foreign traders thought of an alternative medium of payment – opium. Tons of the drug were brought into China from India.

A Ming masterpiece: the Nine Dragons screen in Beihai Park, Beijing

In 1839 the Chinese government finally cracked down on this drain on the treasury, which was also causing mass addiction among the Chinese. Some 20,000 chests of opium were confiscated from British merchants in Guangzhou (Canton), and a Qing imperial edict was issued that terminated trade between China and Britain.

Retaliation came a year later in the first of the Opium Wars, which culminated in a series of 'unequal treaties' forced on an increasingly weak Manchu regime. Under the 1842 Treaty of Nanjing, China was obliged to pay an indemnity to Britain, to open major ports to foreign political and economic penetration, and to surrender Hong Kong to Britain.

Infinitely more costly in human terms was the Taiping Rebellion, which began in 1850 as a peasant revolt. There was a struggle between the Qing dynasty and rebels determined to overthrow such traditional values as respect for religion, private property and male supremacy. The revolt lasted 14 years and cost more lives than World War I. The Qing finally won, but the regime and the nation would never be the same again.

War with Japan

This became patently clear during the Sino-Japanese War of 1894–5, in which the inadequacy of the Chinese army was starkly displayed. Japan and Western powers were dismantling the Chinese Empire. Demands for reform won the support of the emperor, but his notoriously scheming aunt, the Empress Dowager Cixi (Tz'u Hsi), edged him off the throne. Soon after, Cixi had the chance to exploit the Boxer Rebellion (1900), a revolt against foreign influence. It was finally put down by the intervention of all the great powers, which joined together in an unprecedented alliance. China was saddled with the payment of a humiliating indemnity and a further loss of respect.

The elderly empress died in 1908, one day after the mysterious death of her nephew, the unseated emperor. The heir apparent was a two-year-old prince, Puyi – hardly the leader the dynasty and the nation needed in the face of civil disorder and foreign threats.

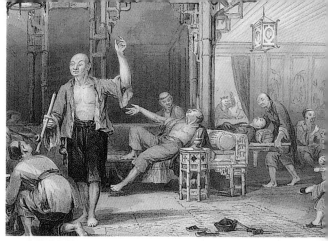

A Guangzhou opium den: addiction was rife in the 19th century

Less than three years later, an army uprising took place in Wuhan and quickly won widespread support. The success of the revolution surprised many observers. It came so suddenly that Dr Sun Yat-sen, the inveterate revolutionary who had led several earlier insurrections, was still abroad at the time. He returned in triumph to accept the presidency of the Chinese Republic. The Manchu dynasty and its child-emperor surrendered in 1911. Puyi continued to live in the Imperial Palace (Forbidden City) in Beijing until 1924, but the rule of the Sons of Heaven on the Dragon Throne, which had begun 4,000 years earlier, had come to an end.

But the path of the new republic was strewn with dangers. A warlord seized power in Beijing, hoping to restore the monarchy. A harried Sun Yat-sen then moved his new Guomindang (Nationalist Party) south to Guangzhou. Towards the end of hostilities, China entered World War I on the side of the Allies. But the Versailles Peace conference proved a bitter disappointment when Japan, and not China, won control over Germany's former holdings in Shandong Province. Frustration inspired protest demonstrations. The targets of increasing bitterness were the foreign powers and the regime in Beijing, as agitation for drastic social reforms caught the imagination of students and factory workers.

In 1921, the Communist Party of China (with a total membership of 53) held its first national congress, in secret, in Shanghai. A cautious communist alliance was arranged with the Guomindang in 1924. Disappointed with the Western powers, Sun Yat-sen turned for support to the leaders of the young Soviet regime. The Kremlin obliged by sending political and military advisors. In turn, Dr Sun dispatched his 37-year-old follower, Chiang Kai-shek, as head of a mission to Moscow. Dr Sun, who rallied the Chinese with his Three Principles – Nationalism, Democracy and the People's Livelihood – died in 1925. His successor, Chiang Kai-shek, took over the campaign, moving the capital to Nanjing.

In 1927 Chiang turned on the communists as well as on leftists within his own party, unleashing a vehement, bloody purge. The communists, who had already organised the support of millions of peasants, gathered strength in the south. But, facing increasing military pressure, they set forth on the epic Long March to northwest China, a distance of some 10,000 perilous kilometres (over

---

Historical Footprints

Even today, you occasionally see old Chinese women hobbling along on deformed feet – living relics of the feudal practice of foot-binding. As early as the Song Dynasty, nearly 1,000 years ago, the preference for women with small feet took a sinister turn. Small girls had their feet broken, turned under, then bandaged to prevent them from growing. The fact that they were in excruciating pain and could never again walk normally seemed secondary to the potential appeal of 'three-inch feet'. It also kept the women effectively in their place, virtually house-bound. At first, it was practised by only the very rich, who regarded it as a status symbol. Over the years, the practice spread to even poor farming families. Foot-binding was outlawed from time to time, but generally remained a fact of Chinese life over the centuries. It began to die out only after the fall of the monarchy in 1911.

6,200 miles). During one of history's greatest strategic retreats, one of the founders of the Chinese Communist Party, Mao Zedong (Mao Tse-tung), was chosen as party leader. It was a mandate he was to retain for the rest of his life.

The Bitter Years of War

In 1931 Manchuria was seized by Japan and then proclaimed as the 'independent' state of Manchukuo. This was to be a fatal prologue to World War II. Over the next few years Japanese troops advanced into several other areas of northern

Heroes of the Republic: Sun Yatsen and his wife Song Qing Ling

China. The government of Chiang Kai-shek was so busy tracking communists that the Japanese foe merited only casual attention. At one point Chiang himself was kidnapped by some of his own officers, a sensational interlude known as the Sian (Xi'an) Incident. Its aim was to convince him to unite with the communists.

But by the time concerted action could be planned, the invaders had moved on to a broad offensive. The Japanese juggernaut crushed all the resistance in the big coastal cities as well as in Beijing and Nanjing. The retreat ended in 1938 with the nationalist government dug in behind the gorges of the Yangzi River, in the last-ditch capital of Chongqing.

Even before entering World War II, the US was supporting the armies of Chiang Kai-shek with food, fuel and transport. However, once in the field, the Americans soon became disheartened with the confusion, corruption and stalling. Chiang, they believed, was hoarding everything from rice to aircraft in the struggle against the Chinese communists and leaving the Allies to worry about the Japanese.

The Communist Party held its first congress in this Shanghai house

When Japan surrendered in 1945, Chiang Kai-shek could share the victory toasts as one of the Allies. But he was already losing the battle of his lifetime – for China. By V-J Day (15 August), when Japan officially surrendered, the Chinese communists controlled an area inhabited by nearly one-quarter of the nation's population. At first the Americans tried to mediate between the communists and the nationalists, even while continuing to supply the nationalists. But any chances for post-war co-operation between right and left were wrecked in a matter of months. China was sinking into civil war.

Despite early setbacks, the communist armies became an overwhelming force. They were greeted as liberators by the peasants and met only desultory resistance in most cities. The nationalists, in despair, fell back and finally fled, moving the government and countless national treasures to the island of Taiwan, pledging to return one day.

In Tiananmen Square in Beijing on 1 October 1949, Chairman Mao Zedong proclaimed Zhonghua Renmin Gongheguo – the People's Republic of China. After thousands of years of empire and a few decades of violent transition, the most populous country in the world was committed to communism.

Imposing the New Order

Before any grandiose plans could be implemented, China's fledgling rulers had to rebuild society and a crippled economy.

Agrarian reform was the first revolutionary innovation, followed by organisation of the cities under Party control.

Hardly had the groundwork been laid than China entered the Korean War, sending 'volunteers' to fight against American-led United Nations forces. Relations between the US and China suffered, but Beijing's ties with Moscow prospered in comradely harmony. The world's first communist state, the USSR, shipped technical advisors and roubles to China, and many new institutions were set up along Soviet lines. As in Russia, the farms were collectivised and heavy industry took economic precedence.

Mao Zedong's 'Great Leap Forward' (1959) was designed as a crash programme of economic growth, but it kept the country in turmoil and brought unconvincing results. At about the time the Leap was suddenly reversed, relations between China and the Soviet Union plunged from polite to frosty to hostile. China cut off relations with the world and tested its own nuclear bomb.

From 1966 to 1976, China was convulsed by the Great Proletarian Cultural Revolution. This was Mao's attempt to put an end to bureaucratic stagnation and the degeneration of the Chinese Revolution. He saw students as his activists and encouraged them to turn on their teachers. The most chaotic phase lasted from May 1966 until late 1967. Students organised 'Red Guard' units all over China. Mao's slogan that 'It is right to rebel' propelled their campaign to destroy remnants of the old society. Brandishing Mao's *Little Red Book* of quotations, they destroyed temples and historic sites, and

New laws to bring equality for women and make divorce possible seemed, in theory, like true progress. In reality, women had to hold full-time jobs in addition to maintaining the home.

broke into homes to destroy books and art. Much of China's cultural heritage was destroyed. Party leaders and other 'counter-revolutionary' forces were denounced and subjected to mass trials.

Changes came in quick succession in the 1970s. In 1971 China was admitted to the United Nations. In 1972, the US president, Richard Nixon, visited China, thus paving the way to normalising relations between the two countries. In early 1976 the widely admired prime minister, Zhou Enlai, died. Eight months later, in September, death came to Chairman Mao himself.

The Republic after Mao

Mao's widow, the one-time film actress Jiang Qing, and her close associates (the so-called 'Gang of Four') were arrested, tried and imprisoned. Accused of a wide variety of crimes, they served as convenient scapegoats for the havoc of the Cultural Revolution. Thousands who had suffered during the fervent 1960s and 1970s, including the forceful pragmatist Deng Xiaoping, were rehabilitated. In 1978 Deng became China's paramount leader and inaugurated what he called a 'second revolution'. He stressed the 'Four Modernisations' – in agriculture, industry, national defence, and science and technology – for Chinese development. Mao had considered politics the key to China's progress. Deng put his faith in economic advances.

Relations with the United States were normalised in 1979. Deng travelled to the US and met President Jimmy Carter and congressional and business leaders. Deng's policy of 'opening' China to the outside was a recognition that the country needed technological expertise and capital from elsewhere.

To modernise agriculture, Deng disbanded Mao's communes, which had proved over the decades to be a disaster. Farmers could now sell surplus vegetables, fruit, fish or poultry in private markets and keep the profits. As a result, rural agricultural production more than doubled in the 1980s. Deng began reforming industry in China by upgrading outdated technology and managerial systems, implementing price reforms, promoting foreign trade and investment, revamping the banking system and encouraging private business. Later, he even introduced limited stock markets.

Of the 'Gang of Four', Jiang Qing and Zhang Chunqiao received suspended death sentences; Wang Hongwen was sentenced to life, and Yao Wenyuan to a 20-year term.

Contemporary China

In April 1989, Tiananmen Square became the focus of the world's media, as students and workers aired their grievances against the government after reformer Hu Yaobang's death. Angered by widespread corruption, they demanded democratic reform. As the number of protesters swelled to a million, martial law was imposed, and, on the night of 3 June and early hours of 4 June, the army stormed Tiananmen Square. Although debate continues concerning bloodshed in the square itself, at least 300 people are believed to have died in surrounding streets. The incident provoked international outrage and also showed that China's leadership would not tolerate political challenge in any form.

Chairmain Mao gazes out towards Tiananmen Square

Despite crushing China's democracy movement, the government knew that its survival depended on both absolute power and the continuing success of its economic reform. The 1990s were a decade of rampant economic growth as well as tension between China and other nations, as Deng's successor, Jiang Zemin, grappled with China's new role in the international community.

Hong Kong returned to China in 1997 and Macau in 1999. Attention turned to Taiwan, which Beijing hoped to woo back to the fold, promising 'one country, two systems'. To date, Taiwan has resisted reunification while shying away from declaring independence. Cross-straits relations became increasingly strained after the 2000 election (and 2004 re-election) of pro-independence President Chen Shui-bian.

US–China relations have improved since September 11 2001, although this has been marred by several factors: US support for Taiwan; US criticism of China's human rights record; the 1999 bombing of the Chinese Embassy in Belgrade; and the collision in 2001 between a US spy plane and a Chinese fighter aircraft off China's south coast. In 2001 China joined the World Trade Organisation, and in 2003 Hu Jintao succeeded Jiang Zemin as president and Wen Jiabao replaced Zhu Rongji as premier, completing the shift to a younger leadership.

Since the millennium's turn, China has undergone amazing economic growth. In 2004 the mainland's GDP grew 9.5 percent, sustaining pace in 2005. Under its WTO obligations, the government has slowly been opening the economy to foreign players and developing the stock markets. Friendship stores have been replaced by the likes of Wal-Mart, Carrefour and Ikea. Many people in the cities of the eastern coastal regions and the south have become wealthy, but progress has been slow to reach the countryside, and the rich–poor divide has widened. Farmers struggle with corrupt local government and loss of land, while many workers are left jobless from defunct state-owned enterprises. While life seems freer – you can discuss any issues with friends, travel abroad, watch once banned movies – the government retains tight control of the media and the internet, blocking sites and monitoring internet cafes.

Prosperous Hong Kong returned to China in 1997

Historical Highlights

21st–16th centuries BC Xia dynasty: the first Chinese state.

16th–11th centuries BC Shang dynasty. Bronze casting.

11th–5th centuries BC Zhou dynasty. Capital established at Chang'an.

771BC Zhou capital moved to Luoyang.

551BC Birth of Confucius.

475–221BC Conflict between the 'Warring States'.

221–206BC Qin dynasty. Construction of the Great Wall.

206BC–AD220 Han dynasty. International trade along the Silk Road.

220AD Three Kingdoms. First mention of tea-drinking.

265–420 Jin dynasty. Luoyang's temples and palaces destroyed by invaders.

386–581 Northern dynasties. Construction of the Datong Buddhist caves.

420–589 Southern dynasties. China invaded by Huns and Turks.

581–618 Sui dynasty. Printing invented. Grand Canal construction begins.

618–907 Tang dynasty. Invention of gunpowder and porcelain.

907–960 'Five Dynasties and Ten Kingdoms'.

960–1280 Song dynasty. Movable-type printing and paper money.

1279–1368 Yuan (Mongol) dynasty. Beijing the capital. Marco Polo in China.

1368–1644 Ming dynasty. Imperial Palace built in Beijing.

1644–1911 Qing dynasty (Manchu). Rebellions and Opium Wars.

1911–49 Republic of China under Sun Yat-sen then Chiang Kai-shek.

1934–35 Communists abandon southern China: the Long March.

1938–45 Japanese invasion and World War II.

1945–49 Civil war between nationalists and communists.

1949 Revolution: Mao Zedong proclaims the People's Republic.

1966–76 Cultural Revolution.

1976 Mao dies, is succeeded by Deng Xiaoping. He institutes economic reforms and opens China to the West.

1989 Popular demonstration savagely crushed in Tiananmen Square.

1992 Deng restarts economic reforms.

1997 Deng Xiaoping dies, succeeded by Jiang Zemin; Hong Kong reverts from British to Chinese rule.

1999 Macau reverts from Portuguese to Chinese sovereignty.

2001 Beijing is chosen to host the 2008 Olympic Games.

2003 Hu Jintao succeeds Jiang Zemin as president.

WHERE TO GO

The 32 most-visited cities and sights in China, described in detail in this section, are arranged in alphabetical order (omitting Hong Kong and Macau, which are fully explored in their own Berlitz Pocket Guide). This conveniently puts the capital, Beijing, first. The names of the cities and other attractions are given in official *pinyin* spelling. After some place names we provide the spelling by which it was known in the old Wade-Giles system of romanisation: for example, 'Peking' as well as 'Beijing', 'Canton' as well as 'Guangzhou'. There is more on language and pronunciation on page 21 and in the Travel Tips section of this guide *(see page 241)*. At the end of this extended gazetteer, we provide brief notes on 25 additional cities and sights that are less frequently visited on typical tours.

Planning your Trip

Choosing an itinerary can be a difficult task, because China is too big to be covered in any reasonable amount of time. A very hasty week might take in Beijing, the Ming Tombs and the Great Wall; the archaeological marvels of Xi'an; the romantic scenery of Guilin; and a glimpse of bustling Shanghai or Guangzhou. This sort of trip – though you leap around more often than is convenient – takes you to the top attractions.

Less taxing would be a week in and around Shanghai, focusing on the legendary charms of Wuxi, Suzhou and Hangzhou. All three towns are on the historic Grand Canal.

If you venture inland, you can still see the Three Gorges on a two-day cruise between Chongqing and Yichang. The journey conveys you through the gorges (before they are diminished in size after the completion of the Three Gorges Dam in 2009), and from Yichang you can fly to Beijing, Shanghai or Guangzhou for sightseeing, shopping and Chinese cuisine.

The Great Wall winds sinuously from the Yellow Sea to the Gobi Desert

Silk Road enthusiasts fly from Beijing or Xi'an to Urumqi in the far west, returning via the exotic desert oases of Turpan and Dunhuang for the Buddhist cave treasures and camel rides to sand-locked lakes.

Another western China adventure is a visit to Yunnan Province, whose capital, Kunming, is home to members of many of China's minority groups. Nearby is the Stone Forest, a natural monument of bizarre formations, and to the northwest, towards the Burmese and Tibetan borders, are the dazzling minority villages of Dali and Lijiang.

If you prefer to stay close to Beijing, the better part of a varied week could be spent investigating the carvings of the Buddhist caves near Datong, visiting the Mongolian grasslands north of Hohhot, and viewing the Chinese and Tibetan temples of Chengde. Any of these segments can be combined for a longer tour. Popular itineraries invariably include Beijing, Xi'an, Guilin and Shanghai, each city providing a glimpse of China past and present.

Snow on the Hall of Joyful Longevity, Beijing

BEIJING (PEKING)

A visit to the medieval and modern capital of China is an exhausting though rewarding round of palaces and museums, temples and monuments, and streets and stores – a jolting juxtaposition of imperial pomp and contemporary energy.

Beijing has a permanent population of around 12 million, but it is spread over a huge area calculated at a staggering 16,800 sq km (about 6,500 sq miles). Many neighbourhoods of the old city are lined with old *hutong* (alleyways) alongside traditional one- and two-storey courtyard houses (called *siheyuan*), where life has been highly resilient to change. Around the corner from these fast-disappearing cosy alleys are new housing projects, offices, modern shopping plazas and open-air markets. Having secured the 2008 Olympics, the city authorities are busily expanding its subway system, constructing new roads and adding green spaces.

Mostly the city is flat, which is a mercy for the many who cycle to work in the world's most unlikely rush hour, a chaos of buses, trucks and bikes. In the Middle Ages, the emperors decided to do something about the capital's unrelieved flatness. They ordered hills to be built just north of the Forbidden City (at Jingshan) so they could go up and, in total privacy, enjoy a summer breeze and a bird's-eye view over the curved tile roofs of their imperial compound. Try it yourself, perhaps at dawn, when a thin haze drapes itself over the pavilions, redefining yet softening the features of this storybook skyline. You'll see why the emperors wanted it all for themselves.

Beijing in History

Not far from the present-day suburbs of Beijing was the habitat of 'Peking Man', the startling anthropological discovery of the 1920s. A cave near the town of **Zhoukoudian** held the skull of a small-brained but upright ancestor of mankind who lived half a million years ago. Scientists are still sifting for the bones, and visitors can tour the site of the dig.

Mythological beasts on the roof of the Hall of Great Harmony

Excavations in downtown Beijing show that it was inhabited over 20,000 years ago, but the place made little stir until the Warring States period (5th–3rd century BC) when, known as Jicheng, it became the capital of the Kingdom of Yan. Renamed Yanjing, the town served as capital for the Liao dynasty in the 10th century AD. The 12th-century Jin (Chin) dynasty called it Zhongdu ('Central Capital') and built an imperial palace as well as the Lugou Bridge; known abroad as the 'Marco Polo Bridge', it is still in use.

Genghis Khan's Mongol armies levelled Zhongdu in the 13th century, then rebuilt it under the name Dadu ('Great Capital'). By the time Marco Polo arrived, the city outshone the capitals of Europe. The Ming dynasty transferred most of the imperial pomp south to Nanjing in the 14th century. Predictably, Dadu received yet another name, Beiping ('Northern Peace') but had to wait more than 50 years to win back its imperial status and a fresh name. This one – Beijing ('Northern Capital') – is still around. So, happily, are the Ming palaces and temples.

At the beginning of the Qing dynasty, Beijing prospered. New palaces and gardens were laid out and scholarship flourished. A long, slow decline from c.1800 culminated in the Boxer Rebellion of 1900, when European armies wrought havoc in the city in retaliation for the siege of their embassies. This was only the first of many 20th-century crises which were to rock Beijing: the fall of the empire, the foundation of the Chinese Republic, two world wars and civil war. In 1949 Beijing became the capital of the new People's Republic of China.

Sightseeing
The historic heart of Beijing consisted of three concentric cities, rectangular and symmetrical, and a fourth – Outer City – to the south. Most of the miles of walls that protected each of the four cities have been destroyed, but the innermost, Forbidden City, still glitters behind its original fortifications.

The elegance of this city plan, which is basically 700 years old, has never been surpassed. A precise north–south axis links the main elements, from the Bell Tower all the way to the gate of the Outer City, 8km (5 miles) to the south. On either side of the axis, important buildings were laid out as mirror images. Thus Ritan (Altar of the Sun) has its equivalent in Yuetan (Altar of the Moon). Similarly complementary were Xidan and Dongdan, the eastern and western business quarters. At the centre of it all is the Forbidden City, the imperial heart of the Middle Kingdom.

Tiananmen Square
The largest city square on earth, Tiananmen Square covers 40 hectares (100 acres) in the very centre of Beijing. The square was the focus of world attention during the student demonstrations of 1989 and their tragic aftermath. The square is breathtaking in its scale and, despite the brash Communist architecture, affords a pleasant panorama, overflown by kites. At the time of the emperors, the square was only about a quarter its present size. It was expanded in the 1950s to hold up to a million people. In the old, less expansive incarnation Mao Zedong first raised the flag of the new nation on 1 October 1949. Rallies of Red Guards took place here during the Cultural Revolution. On 1 October 1999, the

People's Republic celebrated its golden anniversary here, each of the square's concrete blocks replaced by granite.

The low, squat building at the southern end of the square is the **Chairman Mao Zedong Memorial Hall** (Mao Zhuxi Jiniantang; open Tue–Sun 8–11.30am, Wed and Fri also 2–4pm), contains the embalmed body of the man who led the People's Republic for its first 27 years. The mausoleum, which is bigger than Lenin's tomb in Moscow's Red Square, is open to a procession of tourists, who are allowed only a few minutes inside. Immediately outside the mausoleum, visitors get a graphic picture of how socialism is fast becoming mere consumer kitsch as they are ushered through a small bazaar selling Mao busts, bags, badges and musical lighters playing short renditions of *The East is Red*.

Just to the north is the **Monument to the People's Heroes**, a granite obelisk unveiled in 1958, which is a perfect example of the Socialist Realism style. The democracy movement established its headquarters here in 1989.

On the square's western side, the **Great Hall of the People** (Renmin Dahuitang), erected in 1959, is the grandiose meeting place of the National People's Congress (tours available). Behind is the titanium and glass dome of the **China National Grand Theatre**, set to open in spring 2007, according to media reports.

Across the plaza, to the east, the **National Museum of China** (Zhongguo Guojia Bowuguan, open daily 9am–4pm; entrance fee) comprises two museums in one building. The **Museum of Chinese History** (Zhongguo Lishi Bowuguan) holds 9,000 items from prehistoric fossils to breathtaking pottery and bronzes. The **Museum of the Chinese Revolution** (Zhongguo Geming Bowuguan) houses photographs, paintings, documents and relics from the Communist revolution. The explanations are mainly in Chinese, but you can buy a guide in English from the bookstall to the left of the entrance. Renovation work means that some sections of the museum will be closed until 2007.

North across Chang'an Avenue from Tiananmen Square (and leading to the Forbidden City) is the **Gate of Heavenly Peace**,

The Forbidden City remained closed to ordinary citizens for 500 years

with its famous portrait of Chairman Mao. On top of this formidable stone wall is a rostrum for reviewing parades, and behind it a massive wooden gate-tower with a double roof. The original 15th-century gate complex was rebuilt in 1651. Tourists are now allowed to survey the square from the top of the gate, a vantage point once reserved for emperors and rulers.

Forbidden City (Gu Gong)

Beijing is too sprawling for strolling around, or the sort of browsing that some European cities offer. Among several exceptions, though, is the **Forbidden City** (open daily 8.30am–5pm summer, 8.30am–4.30pm winter; entrance fee). Here you will find more than 72 hectares (175 acres) of grandeur, with palaces, courtyards and gardens.

The Forbidden City, so described because it was off-limits to ordinary people for nearly 500 years, is now called the Imperial Palace Museum (Gu Gong). Designed to contain the auspicious number of 9,999 rooms, its scale is overwhelming and leaves many visitors completely bewildered. Built between 1406 and

One of the bronze lions that watch over the Forbidden City

1420, it was the residence of 24 emperors, their families and their enormous retinues for nearly seven centuries.

Tourists enter the Forbidden City from the south, after a long walk along a cobbled roadway from the Gate of Heavenly Peace. The main entrance to the compound, **Meridian Gate** (Wumen), was designed in the 15th century. Officials used the left portal, members of the imperial family the right. Next comes another ceremonial gate, the **Gate of Supreme Harmony** (Taihemen), first erected in 1420. A pair of monumental bronze lions stand guard.

Beyond this powerful line of defence stands China's supreme ensemble of ancient architecture, three great halls and courtyards that reflect the Three Buddhas and the Three Pure Ones of Daoism. First and foremost is the **Hall of Great Harmony** (Taihedian), popularly called the 'Hall of the Imperial Throne'. This is the biggest building in the Forbidden City and one of China's most beautiful wooden structures. For hundreds of years during the Ming and Qing dynasties this was the tallest building in all Beijing; by law no house could rise higher. (Counting the hall's upswept roof decorations, that meant the limit was approximately 37.5m, or 123ft.) Inside, on a raised platform, the 'Son of Heaven' sat on his Dragon Throne surrounded by symbols of longevity and power and cowering acolytes, all covered in a fog of incense. To the tune of gongs and chimes, visitors knelt to kowtow nine times. This is the

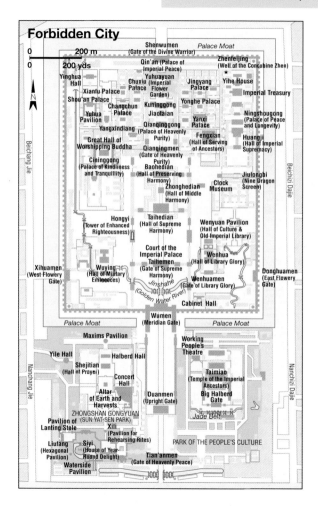

Forbidden City

0 _____ 200 m

0 _____ 200 yds

N

Beichang Jie

Shenwumen
(Gate of the Divine Warrior)   Palace Moat

Zhenfeijing
(Well of the Concubine Zhen)

Qin'an (Palace of
Imperial Peace)

Yinghua
Hall

Yuhuayuan
(Imperial
Flower
Garden)

Chuxiu
Palace

Jingyang
Palace

Yihe House

Xianfu Palace

Shou'an Palace

Changchun
Palace

Kuninggong
Jiaotaian

Yonghe Palace

Imperial Treasury

Yuhua
Pavilion

Qianqinggong
(Palace of Heavenly
Purity)

Yanxi
Palace

Ningshougong
(Palace of Peace
and Longevity)

Yangxindiang

Great Hall of
Worshipping Buddha

Qianqingmen
(Gate of Heavenly
Purity)

Fengxian
(Hall of Serving
of Ancestors)

Huangji
(Hall of Imperial
Supremacy)

Cininggong
(Palace of Kindliness
and Tranquillity)

Baohedian
(Hall of Preserving
Harmony)

Zhonghedian
(Hall of Middle
Harmony)

Clock
Museum

Jiulongbi
(Nine Dragon
Screen)

Hongyi
(Tower of Enhanced
Righteousness)

Taihedian
(Hall of Supreme
Harmony)

Wenyuan Pavilion
(Hall of Culture &
Old Imperial Library)

Court of the
Imperial Palace

Taihemen
(Gate of Supreme
Harmony)

Wuying
(Hall of Military
Eminences)

Wenhua
(Hall of Library Glory)

Xihuamen
(West Flowery
Gate)

Jinshahe
(Golden Water River)

Wenhuamen
(Gate of Library Glory)

Donghuamen
(East Flowery
Gate)

Cabinet Hall

Wumen
(Meridian Gate)

Palace Moat   Palace Moat

Maxims Pavilion

Working
People's
Theatre

Yile Hall

Halberd Hall

Shejitian
(Hall of Prayer)

Taimiao
(Temple of the Imperial
Ancestors)

Concert
Hall

Duanmen
(Upright Gate)

Big Halberd
Gate

Altar
of Earth and
Harvests

ZHONGSHAN GONGYUAN
(SUN YAT-SEN PARK)

Jade Belt

Pavilion of
Lanting Stele

Xili
(Pavilion for
Rehearsing Rites)

PARK OF THE PEOPLE'S CULTURE

Liufang
(Hexagonal
Pavilion)

Siyi
(House of Year-
Round Delight)

Tian'anmen
(Gate of Heavenly Peace)

Waterside
Pavilion

Beichang Jie

Nanchang Jie

Nanchizi Dajie

Beichizi Dajie

place where the most solemn ceremonies, such as the New Year rites or the enthronement of a new emperor, were held.

Less formal occasions took place in the smaller, golden-roofed **Hall of Central Harmony** (Zhonghedian), behind the Hall of Great Harmony. A third hall in this series, the **Hall of Preserving Harmony** (Baohedian), was used for, among other things, the palace examinations, which were the world's first civil-service tests. Behind this hall, in the centre of a stairway, is a ramp full of sculptured dragons carved from a single slab of marble weighing more than 200 tonnes. The stairway was reserved for the passage of the emperor's sedan chair. Thousands of labourers worked to pull the block to this site from the quarry 48km (30 miles) away; ingeniously, the operation was scheduled for deepest winter so that the load could be slid along specially iced roads.

From here to the north, the density of structures in the Forbidden City increases markedly as one passes from the Outer Court (where official business was conducted) to the halls and pavilions of the Inner Court (where the emperor, the imperial family and court members lived).

> **For nearly 2,000 years, the Chinese emperors required that their male servants be eunuchs, in order to protect their concubines. The Ming court would have contained up to 20,000. Even in 1911, the eunuch population in the Qing Forbidden City was as high as 1,000.**

Many of the old palaces and halls are now used to display the artwork and more prosaic belongings of the emperors. The **Clock Museum** and **Imperial Treasury**, collections of gifts to the emperors, are worth a detour to the right, as is the magnificent **Nine-Dragon Screen** (Jiulongbi), carved in 1775.

The rear (northern) section of the Forbidden City ends at the **Imperial Gardens** (Yuhua-yuan), with magnificent stone rockeries, site of a Daoist temple that dates back to the completion of the Forbidden City itself under the Ming emperors in 1420.

Parks and Pavilions

Just north of the Forbidden City complex, along the main imperial axis, is **Jingshan Park**, formerly known as Coal Hill (open daily 6am–9pm; entrance fee). The highest point of old Beijing, the hill was created from earth that was originally removed to form the moat system around the Forbidden City. Each of the five artificial peaks was provided with a romantically designed pavilion. The three-tiered **Pavilion of Ten Thousand Springs** (Wanchunting), on the middle peak, offers an inspiring view over the glistening rooftops of the Imperial City, with the modern capital just beyond.

The White Dagoba, or Baita, in Beihai Park

Beihai Park (open daily 6.30am–8pm; entrance fee), Beijing's favourite, has been a beauty spot for many hundreds of years. Its lake, which young couples now explore in rented rowing boats, was created in the 12th century. The graceful Bridge of Eternal Peace (Yonganqiao) leads to an artificial island a mile in circumference with a long covered corridor that sweeps along the northern shore. On a hill in the centre of the isle is situated a Tibetan-style stupa, the **White Dagoba** (Baita), at the back of Yongan Temple. It was built in 1651 to commemorate the first visit of the Dalai Lama to Beijing, and stands on the site of Kublai Khan's winter palace. In springtime the dagoba seems to burst from waves of green leaves. In summer and autumn, this is the most beautiful and lively park to stroll through in the capital.

Temple of Heaven Park

Tiantan Park, known to foreigners as Temple of Heaven Park (open daily 8am–6pm; entrance fee), is the biggest of Beijing's parks, celebrated for its assembly of thrilling 15th-century architecture. The highlight is the circular, blue tile-roofed **Hall of Prayer for Good Harvest** (Qiniandian). This marvel of geometry, art and engineering, built of wood without a single nail, measures 37.5m (123ft) to the gilded orb on its topmost roof. In 1889 the masterpiece was struck by lightning and burnt almost to the ground. Fortunately, the ruin was quickly restored to its original, resplendent state.

At the winter solstice, the emperor expressed thanks here for the previous harvest then, on the 15th day of the first lunar month of the year, he was carried here in a procession to pray to the gods of sun and moon, clouds and rain for a bountiful harvest in the year to come. The floor plan of the hall provides the key to the building's function. The four central columns represent the seasons; then come two concentric rings of 12 columns each, representing the months and the dozen 2-hour periods into which the day was divided; and 28 hardwood pillars symbolise the constellations.

Although tourists can no longer enter this monument, its colourful interiors can still be glimpsed from outside. Other attractions at the park include the **Round Altar** (Yuanqiu) – three tiers of balustrades with 360 pillars representing the days of the lunar year – and **Echo Wall**, where whispers ricochet and are mysteriously magnified, crossing an immense courtyard, without benefit of modern technology.

This park is the best place in Beijing to observe practitioners of tai chi at their morning exercise, or calligraphers at work, or people flying kites, playing badminton or traditional music, or even practising ballroom dancing.

Top Temples

Beijing's most popular temple is a 17th-century Lamasery, the **Palace of Harmony and Peace** (Yonghegong), popularly known as the Lama Temple (open daily 9am–4.30pm; entrance fee). It

The wooden Lama Temple has been spectacularly restored

was originally the palace of the prince who became the Emperor Yongzheng. The stately complex of wooden buildings, containing nearly 1,000 rooms, has been painstakingly restored. The temple recalls 18th-century efforts to unify China, Mongolia and Tibet.

Across the street and down a narrow lane from the Lama Temple is Beijing's most serene place of worship, the **Temple of Confucius** (Miao Kong; open daily 9am–4.30pm; entrance fee), with statues and stone tablets honouring the ancient sage. This was where emperors came to offer sacrifices to Confucius for guidance in ruling the empire. Built in 1306, it is the second largest Confucian temple in China, after the one in Confucius' home tome, Qufu.

Other temples of significant interest and variety are the **Big Bell Temple** (Dazhongsi; open daily 8.30am–4pm; entrance fee), with China's leading collection of antique bells; the **Temple of the White Pagoda** (Baitasi; open daily 8.30am–4.30pm), with its 13th-century Tibetan stupa and excellent collection of Buddhist statues; the **Five Pagoda Temple** (Wutasi; open daily 8.30am–4.30pm), decorated with Indian-influenced sculptures; and the **White Clouds Daoist Temple** (Baiyunguan; open daily

8.30am–4.30pm; entrance fee), where Beijingers of all ages crowd in to pray for good fortune at a variety of most unusual shrines.

An Ancient Observatory, Zoo and Aquarium

The **Ancient Observatory** (Gu Guanxiangtai; open daily 9am–4pm; entrance fee) was built in 1442 and stands on top of a remnant of the old city wall near one of the busiest intersections in central Beijing (where Jianguomenwai Dajie meets the 2nd Ring Road). Many of the bronze instruments, sundials and sextants on display inside and on the roof of the observatory were gifts from Jesuit missionaries who lived in the capital in the 17th century.

Beijing Zoo (Beijing Dongwuyuan; open summer 7.30am–6pm; winter 7.30am–5.30pm; entrance fee), in the northwest of the city, is the largest in China. It now includes a separate indoor-outdoor pavilion for its lovable giant pandas. The older buildings (dating back to the Qing dynasty) house Manchurian tigers, Tibetan yaks, snow leopards and Père David's deer, known to the Chinese as the sibuxiang ('quadruple unlikeness')

Labyrinth of Lanes

In old Beijing, the principal streets divided the city into a grid, in which each square section was filled with a network of lanes, or *hutong* (from the Mongolian *hut* or horse trough. Between the lanes, square single-storey houses were built around a central courtyard, with few outward-facing windows and one wooden gate, which often had carved characters intended to bring good fortune to the house owner or his trade. The houses were built so close together that the lanes were just wide enough for a rider on horseback. The name of each *hutong* tells its story by describing the life it contained. Some indicate professions or crafts: Bowstring Makers' Lane, Cloth Lane, Hat Lane. Some lanes, if they were inhabited by a single family, carry the family name. The best areas to see *hutong* are Qianmen (south of Tiananmen Square) and around the Bell and Drum towers (north of Beihai Park).

because it has characteristics of the deer, the reindeer, the ox and the donkey. The zoo is popular with local children, but most foreign visitors find the facilities antiquated and its conditions poor.

Rather than upgrade its aged facilities, Beijing Zoo opened the **Beijing Aquarium**, also China's largest, on adjacent property (open summer 9am–6pm; winter 9am–5pm; entrance fee). Home to whales, dolphins and 50,000 fish, the

One of Beijing's traditional quarters, Qianmen Dajie

huge conch-shaped facility also features a 'Touch Tidepool', sea mammals shows and some of the world's largest viewing panels.

Hutong and Courtyards

Growing in popularity in the face of extinction by bulldozer, the *hutong* (traditional alleyways) and courtyard houses of Beijing are worth a visit. Every year these old neighbourhoods are reduced as the capital relentlessly reconstructs itself, but you can still book a guided pedicab tour of the *hutong*. Traversing the backstreets in the old lake district north of Beihai Park, these pedicab caravans make stops at the ancient **Drum Tower** (Gulou; open daily 9am–4.30pm) for panoramic views over the courtyard houses, at **Prince Gong's Palace** (Gongwangfu) for tea and sometimes opera in a lavish grand Ming dynasty estate, and at a typical courtyard home in a *hutong* neighbourhood for a chance to meet and talk with Beijing residents.

If time allows for further exploration of these old neighbourhoods, have a look around Qianhai and Houhai lakes for weekend street markets. Here you'll find **Songqingling Guzhu**, the former home of Song Qing Ling (the second wife of modern China's founder, Dr Sun Yat-sen), who lived in this courtyard mansion after the revolution. The building is now a family museum (open Tues–Sun 9am–4.30pm).

Shopping Districts

Some of Beijing's few walkable areas are its chief shopping streets and markets. **Wangfujing**, running north a few blocks east of the Forbidden City, is the capital's primary shopping street, lined with up-market boutiques and glittering shopping plazas, although a few venerable arts and crafts shops, small galleries and old department stores still survive. Southwest of Tiananmen Square is Liulichang, a shopping street

> The narrowest lane in Beijing is Qianshi Hutong, just 38cm (15in) wide at it narrowest point. The shortest is Yichi Dajie, 9m (30ft) from end to end.

that has been restored to its Ming dynasty appearance and is Beijing's premier antiques market. It extends eastwards into Dazhalan Street, a pedestrian mall famous for silk and jewellery.

Tough haggling skills are essential at Silk Alley (Xishui Shichang), which has several floors of copycat 'designer' clothing. In 2005 Gucci, Prada, Chanel and some other luxury brands sued the manager of Silk Alley for alleged piracy. An excellent range of clothes can be found on the five floors of the Sanlitun Yaxiu Clothing Market. The Hongqiao Market, just to the east of the Temple of Heaven, features clothing, crafts (including antique clocks) and freshwater pearls. For traditional Chinese paintings, calligraphy supplies and rare books, poke around Liulichang *(see above)*. The most colourful market is Panjiayuan (known as the Dirt Market), starting at sunrise every day but closing around 4pm, with its stalls of collectables, antiques, family treasures, tomb art, Tibetan rugs, furniture and Mao memorabilia. Prices can be low here, if you bargain.

The Summer Palace

The Chinese name for this convergence of natural and man-made beauty is **Yiheyuan** – the 'Park of Nurtured Harmony' (open daily 6.30am–6pm; entrance fee). Foreigners call this 280-hectare (700-acre) imperial estate the **Summer Palace**. In actual fact, the 250-year-old palaces, pavilions, temples and halls occupy only a small part of the dreamily landscaped area. By far the largest feature of the park is Kunming Lake.

Contemporary Chinese historians wax indignant that, under the Qing dynasty, funds intended for the imperial navy were siphoned off to make Yiheyuan an increasingly luxurious private park. Perhaps the most astonishing item on which the Empress Dowager Cixi squandered the naval budget is a double-decker **Marble Boat** beached at the edge of the lake. You can view this monument to royal folly, but you can no longer board it.

Among the outstanding structures in the park are the Hall of Joyful Longevity (Leshoutang) and the Seventeen-Arch Bridge, but the most magnificent structure is the **Long Corridor**, a wooden gallery 728m (nearly half a mile) in length, running

The Pavilion of Precious Clouds in the Summer Palace

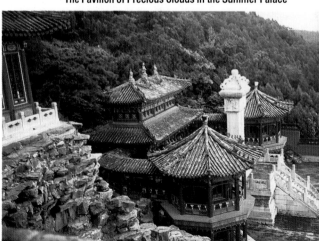

parallel to the northern shore of the lake and linking the scattered palace buildings. This covered way, which is interrupted by octagonal pavilions, is decorated with landscape paintings and depictions of Chinese legends. It's like a long, unfolding wooden scroll of Old Cathay, a lakeside gallery recording all that was once the Middle Kingdom.

A few kilometres from the Summer Palace is the **Old Summer Palace** (Yuanmingyuan), which was once the emperor's summer retreat. In 1860 British and French soldiers attacked and destroyed most of the grand buildings, including a complex modelled after Versailles. Today, the ghostly ruins make an idyllic place to enjoy a picnic.

Excursions from Beijing

The area surrounding Beijing has some interesting locales that attract visitors hoping to spend time away from the chaos of the capital. Transport by train or bus is readily available and convenient, though for shorter trips such as the Great Wall and the Ming Tombs, a hired car may be easiest. Travel agents can also help to arrange such trips.

> The top of the Great Wall was designed so that five or six horsemen could ride side by side, between the crenellated walls. Fortified towers, signal beacon towers and garrisons completed the defences.

The Great Wall

It is about 80km (50 miles) from the centre of Beijing northwest to the most visited stretch of the **Great Wall of China**, at **Badaling**. The trip telescopes history, from the modern capital through the outskirts where donkey carts and cargo-carrying bicycles share the road, past farms where nothing seems to have changed for centuries, to a harsh mountain range where nearly one million workers walled in an empire. Like all the real wonders of the world, this one is more awesome when visited in person than it is in any film or book.

The first elements of the wall system were built more than 2,000 years ago, but the expansion and consolidation of the project near Beijing began under the Ming dynasty in the 14th century. The serpentine stone bulwark and elevated highway became Wanlichangcheng – 'The Wall Ten Thousand Li Long' (about 6,000km/3,700 miles).

The restored section of the wall at Badaling, undulating up the unexpectedly steep hillsides, can be a test of endurance. It is far steeper and more formidable than it looks in any tourist brochure. Out of breath, many visitors exchange sympathetic smiles along the way as they ascend

The Great Wall at Simatai has hardly been restored

to one or another of the towers. If you walk far enough west, you reach dilapidated and unrestored sections of the wall that trail off into the distance.

The Badaling section is often overcrowded these days, and there are countless stalls selling tacky souvenirs. Two other sections now provide relatively easy access to tourists: the Great Wall at **Mutianyu**, as beautiful as the section at Badaling but a little less steep, and the Great Wall at **Simatai**, more distant from Beijing (100km/60 miles to the northeast) than other sections but virtually unrestored. Simatai is the least crowded and most original of the Great Wall sites. Although it too has a cable-car concession, Simatai bills itself as 'the most dangerous section of the Great Wall'. As access improves, more sections of the Wall are opening up to tourism, such as at Huanghuacheng and Jinshaling.

The Ming Tombs

On the way to the Great Wall is the peaceful valley the Ming emperors chose as their burial ground. In 1407 the Emperor Yongle ordered a search for a suitable burial place with auspicious 'wind and water' conditions, as well as appropriate grandeur. This site proved so perfect that all but three of the succeeding Ming rulers were entombed in the same valley.

The route to the 13 **Ming Tombs** (Shisan Ling; open daily 8am–5.30pm; entrance fee) begins at a great marble gateway more than four centuries old. Beyond this is the main gate with three archways; the middle arch was used only once in each reign – for the delivery of the emperor's remains to his tomb.

One of the stone warriors guarding the Sacred Way

Then comes the **Sacred Way** (Shendao), which is flanked by 36 enormous stone guardians. There are a dozen military and civil dignitaries and a dozen pairs of animals, real and mythical, including lions, camels, elephants, unicorns and chimeras.

The largest tomb (Changling) belonged to Yongle himself. Its Hall of Eminent Favours (Lingendian) is Beijing's largest wooden structure remaining from ancient times. The 32 gilded pillars supporting the coffered ceiling were fashioned from a huge tree that took more than five years to ship here from southwest China. The tomb itself has not been excavated. and the emperor and empress still lie undisturbed within the vaults.

Ninety-one steps lead down below ground level to Dingling (the tomb of the Emperor Wanli, who reigned from 1573 to 1620). It took 30,000 workers six years to build this underground palace, the only tomb on this site to have been excavated. Most of the regalia and artefacts on display, including the wooden coffin containers, are copies of the items excavated in the 1950s.

An elaborate headdress discovered in the Ming Tombs

The Eastern Qing Tombs

While many visitors to the Ming Tombs find the site rather crowded and uninspiring, there is a fascinating alternative. The **Eastern Qing Tombs** (Dongqingling; open daily 8.30am–5pm; entrance fee) mimic the older Ming architecture but are grander and more effectively restored. They are also more than twice as far from Beijing: 125km (78 miles) to the east on slow but interesting roads. Of the nine tombs open to view, those of the two most powerful Manchu emperors, Qianlong and Kangxi, are impressive, and that of Empress Dowager Cixi (1835–1911) is as elaborate as it is strange.

CHANGSHA

If you go to Changsha by train, you will arrive at the second-biggest railway station in China, a distinction quite out of proportion to the amount of rail traffic or the size of the city. The explanation is that, until the late 1970s, legions of pilgrims converged on this provincial capital in search of the roots of Chairman Mao Zedong. Now that the cult of Mao has faded in glory, despite recurrent revivals of interest, Changsha has returned to its age-old role as a rather prosaic regional centre of trade and

A pavement cobbler repairs shoes in the centre of Changsha

culture. However, the surrounding fertile countryside is attractive, the spicy Hunan cuisine is worth trying, the scenic mountain areas of the province are outstanding and the archaeological displays are stunning.

The capital of Hunan Province, Changsha lies along the Xiang River, a wide and often turbulent stream that flows into the Yangzi. The long thin strip of **Orange Island** (Juzizhou), rich in oranges among other crops, bisects the river and in the early 20th century was home to a small band of Western traders and missionaries. From the pavilion at the southern tip there is an engrossing view of sampans, barge trains and passenger ships.

On the far side of the river, fragrant forests climb the slopes of **Yuelu Hill**, a favourite escape from the subtropical heat of the city in summer. The yew tree standing in front of the mountainside **Lushan Temple** is said to be more than 1,700 years old. The Qing dynasty pavilion on top affords a fine panorama.

For most tourists the prime attraction of the region is found in the northeast part of town: the **Hunan Provincial Museum** (Hunan Bowuguan; open daily 9am–noon and 2.30–5pm), with its renowned relics of the Han dynasty, including silks, ceramics and lacquerware of great sophistication, as well as alluring figurines and musical instruments. All these artefacts survived because they were buried in coffins within coffins in subterranean royal tombs. These beautiful wooden boxes come from the royal graves at **Mawangdui**, as does the museum's show-stopper: the remarkably well-preserved silk-wrapped mummy of the Marquis of Dai's wife, Tohou, who died aged 50 in 186BC. Nearly 2,200 years later, her hair is still on her head and her expression is unchanged from the moment of her last breath.

Visitors to Changsha can also see the local embroidery factory, where Hunan's handicraft tradition has flourished for 2,000 years. Artists paint original designs, usually of landscapes, animals, birds or flowers, which the artisans reproduce stitch by microscopic stitch in colourful silk. The workers here are proudest of the double-faced embroidery, with a different picture on each side.

Changsha also features sites linked with Chairman Mao and the revolution. Foremost is Hunan's **No.1 Teachers' Training School** (Diyishifan; open daily 8am–5.30pm). Reconstructed in 1968, it resembles a European monastery, with arcades and gardens. During the Cultural Revolution visitors thronged the institution every day, for this is where Mao Zedong studied from 1913–18 and later taught. The classroom of 30 desks where Mao sat and the crowded dormitory where he slept under a mosquito net are on view.

Shaoshan

Millions of visitors have made the pilgrimage to the village of **Shaoshan**, two hours by bus from Changsha, which was the place of Mao Zedong's birth in 1893. The principal sights are the house where he was born and grew up (Mao Zedong Tongzhi Guju), quite roomy by local standards, and the Museum of Comrade Mao (Mao Zedong Tongzhi Jinianguan) with all the exhibits in duplicate, filling two mirror-image wings designed to double the crowd capacity. Both are open daily 7.30am–5.30pm in summer, 8am–5pm in winter.

Excursions in Hunan

Outdoor enthusiasts and independent travellers might have time to explore two of Hunan's most spectacular natural attractions. The **Southern Heng Mountain** (Hengshannan, also called Nanyue), one of China's Five Sacred Mountains in the ancient Daoist pantheon, is 112km (70 miles) south of Changsha. Its temples, monasteries and misty vistas are well worth a day's hike. Nearby Hengyang, a decent-sized city, is a major hub for rail transport to Guilin and Guangzhou.

Wulingyuan, a large nature reserve better known to the Chinese as Zhangjiajie, is 350km (217 miles) west of Changsha. Known as 'China's Yellowstone', this UNESCO World Heritage Site is a remote park of spectacular beauty. Its landscape is dotted with uncanny quartz labyrinths and pinnacles, massive limestone caves, white-water rapids, steep hiking trails and minority villages. Huangshizhai and Jinbianxi are the most popular areas, with the best scenery and larger numbers of tourists. Most of the more interesting sights are on the walk down; if you don't mind company, it is a good idea to ride the cable car up (daily 8am–6pm) and walk down along with the tour groups.

CHENGDE (JEHOL)

In summer the trip to Chengde, about 250km (150 miles) northeast of Beijing, might well be one of the prettiest anywhere in China. Fertile fields alternate with stony hills, trees and wildflowers. In the hamlets along the way, trim houses are roofed with thatch or traditional tile with winged projections. In the fields, the labour is done mostly by hand, and when animals are not available, even the heavy ploughing is done by men in harness. Chengde itself looks, at first glance, like any other northern Chinese industrial town, but the dreariness is interspersed with beautifully sited old temples and an imperial pleasure-ground big enough to be protected by a wall 10km (6 miles) long – sections of an immense UNESCO World Heritage Site.

The **palaces and gardens** of Chengde provided summertime escape for the imperial courts of the Qing dynasty, beginning with Emperor Kangxi, who created the halls, lakes and hunting grounds here as a second summer palace in 1703. Kangxi was accurate when he called these royal parklands, about 350m (over 1,100ft) above sea level, **Bishushanzhuang** (open daily 5.30am–6.30pm), or 'Mountain Villa for Escaping the Summer Heat'.

His interest in Chengde was strategic as well as recreational, for it strengthened his empire's rule over Mongolians and various frontiers. In line with this strategy, the buildings found in Chengde exhibit an interesting mix of Han and minority architectural styles. Instead of the ornate carvings and large overhanging eaves that characterise Chinese architecture, the summer palace is relatively simple but elegant.

Visitors enter this royal resort at the ceremonial Lizheng Gate, flanked by two marble lions. The old palace and royal halls now serve as museums. Among the exhibits are bows and arrows and

Serenely elegant: the Refreshing Mist-Veiled Waters Pavilion

Chinese flintlocks, rare jade and porcelain, and the sedan chairs in which the emperors were transported all the way from Beijing. The emperor's bedroom is located in the Refreshing Mist-Veiled Waters Pavilion. The halls and courtyards are eminently regal, yet they also inspire a feeling of relaxation appropriate to the setting. The plain wooden corridors connecting the buildings contrast with the illustrated passageways of Beijing's Summer Palace, which occupies just half the space of the Chengde retreat.

The landscape beyond the palace compound features many of the romantic elements of Chinese tradition: interconnected lakes and lotus ponds, forests, causeways and arched bridges, ornate pavilions and towering pagodas. The Tower of Mist and Rain (Yanyulou), a two-storey lakeside pavilion in the southern style, was favoured by emperors for its foggy views resembling those of an old Chinese painting. Tourists can cross the lakes in hand-poled ferryboats or drift at their own pace in a rowing boat. North of the lakes there are hiking trails in the **Garden of Ten Thousand Trees** (Wanshuyuan), where Emperor Qianlong gave an audience in 1793 to the first British ambassador to set foot in China, Lord Macartney. The meeting did not go well.

Beyond the wall surrounding the palace and its gardens rise the exotic roofs of the **Eight Outer Temples**, built by the emperors between 1713 and 1779 to honour and influence Tibetans, Kazakhs and other northern peoples. Most, but not all, are open to tourists. The **Mt Sumeru Longevity and Happiness Temple** (Xumifushoumiao; open daily 8am–5.30pm) replicates the residence in Shigatse, Tibet, of the sixth Panchen Lama, who visited Chengde on the occasion of Qianlong's 70th birthday. It exhibits a blend of Han Chinese and Tibetan architecture. The high red walls surround a pavilion, which has a roof gilded with a ton of gold.

A short distance to the east, the fantastic **Small Potala Temple** (Putuozongchengmiao; open daily 8am–6pm) is the largest at Chengde, a reduced copy of the Potala Palace in Lhasa. The highlight, however, is **Puning Temple** (Puning Si; open 8am–5.30pm) to the northeast, a Chinese and Tibetan-styled temple that houses a colossal, gilded, 22-m (72-ft) high statue of

Guanyin, the Buddhist Goddess of Mercy, carved from five different types of wood.

CHENGDU (CHENGTU)

Balmy, often misty weather keeps Chengdu green and full of flowers year-round. It's the climate in which bamboo thrives, and bamboo is the staple diet of the giant panda. The best place to spot these cuddly-looking beasts in something resembling the wilds is 11km (7 miles) northeast of central Chengdu, at the **Giant Panda Breeding Research Base** (open daily 8am–6pm), where over 40 pandas have free run of some 30 hectares

Chengdu Zoo has more pandas than any other in the world

(80 acres) of bamboo groves. There's a panda museum here, too. In closer confines, the **Chengdu Zoo** (open daily 7.30am–6pm summer, 8am–5.30pm winter) has more resident pandas – about a dozen – than does any other zoo in the world. The thin bamboo stalks they find so delicious are grown right in the grounds. Because they are the stars of this attraction, the giant pandas are assigned high-ceilinged, spacious cages and outdoor play areas.

Chengdu is the capital city of Sichuan (Szechuan) Province, the natural habitat for 80 percent of the world's 1,000 giant pandas. But Chengdu has other attractions as well, some of them historical, some spiritual, and some edible.

At the time of the era of the Three Kingdoms, in the 3rd century, Chengdu was capital of the feudal Kingdom of Shu, and politics, not pandas, was the prime attraction. The principal monument from that era is the **Temple of Marquis Wu** (Wuhousi; open daily 7am–7pm), a complex of halls and gardens in the southern suburbs built to commemorate the kingdom's prime minister. Known in his lifetime (AD181–234) as Zhugeliang, he was posthumously ennobled for his role in unifying the region and developing its economy and culture. In the main hall, built in the Tang dynasty, there are gilt statues of Zhugeliang, his son and his grandson; the latter died in battle at the age of 14.

Chinese literary pilgrims are drawn to another of Chengdu's historic sites, the thatched **cottage of Dufu** (Dufucaotang; open daily 7am–7pm), a shrine, museum and park at the spot where the poet of the Tang dynasty lived in exile from the capital for several years. Dufu (formerly spelled Tufu) lived from 712 to 770 and wrote more than 1,400 poems, many of them regarded as the greatest in the Chinese canon.

Chengdu is famous for its many traditional teahouses

Chengdu's most popular Daoist temple, **Qingyanggong** ('Green Goat Temple'; open daily 6am–8pm) is a lively, garish complex where two bronze 'good luck' goats at the main altar have been rubbed smooth by worshippers seeking their fortunes. Not far away is the centre of Zen (Chan) Buddhism in Sichuan, the 1,300-year-old **Wenshu Temple** (open daily 8.30am–5.30pm), which maintains its own company of woodcarvers as well as a vegetarian restaurant and outdoor teahouse.

Chengdu's largest and most renowned religious monument, located 28km (17 miles) north of the city, is the **Divine Light Monastery** (Baoguangsi; open daily 8am–5pm). The most photographed element of this vast establishment is the stupa, a slightly crooked 13-level pagoda. It was built of stone at the end of the Tang dynasty, replacing an ancient wooden pagoda on the same spot.

The five main halls of the monastery are filled with works of art, including Buddhist sculptures, religious and landscape paintings, and examples of many schools of calligraphy. One 19th-century hall contains 500 larger-than-life-sized statues of Buddhist saints. The 'Ancestor Garden', formerly reserved for retired monks, has been appropriated for the use of foreign tourists only – as a tearoom.

> **The Chongli Pavilion in Wangjianglou was built in memory of Xue Tao, a famous poetess of the Tang dynasty, who used water from the well here to make her paper. She was passionate about bamboos, and organised the planting of the hundred or so varieties still visible in the park.**

By long tradition, Chengdu is China's pre-eminent city of teahouses. Many still operate along the north bank of the Jin ('Brocade') River, serving covered cups of flower tea. Customers linger at courtyard tables, watching trinket vendors and pipe and tobacco salesmen ply their trade along the river promenade, or sometimes enjoying free performances of Sichuan opera or instrumental music.

Another restful spot is **Wangjianglou** (the River Viewing Pavilion Park; open daily 6am–9pm) along the south bank of the Jin River. More than 100 kinds of bamboo grow here. As in other traditional Chengdu parks, there are pavilions and towers, rock gardens, ponds and shady paths. River viewing of a different type is recommended at the site of the **Dujiangyan Irrigation System** (open daily 6am–8pm), 57km (35 miles) northwest of Chengdu. This ambitious irrigation and flood-control project was built around AD256 by Li Bing, the governor of the Shu prefecture. Amazingly, it is still in use, irrigating 2,400 sq km (930 sq miles) of agricultural land. There is a 3-m (10-ft) tall statue of Li Bing in the Pavilion of the Dragon's Defeat (Fulongguan), erected in the 3rd century to commemorate his achievement. The lush hills along the shore provide a poetic setting for an engineering wonder.

In the centre of town some neighbourhoods retain a medieval look. Two-storey shophouses, some sagging with age, line the narrow streets. They have shops on the ground floor and living quarters above, with wooden balconies and distinctive carved designs. But 'progress' is inevitable: on the site of the ancient viceroy's palace, in the very centre of Chengdu, a giant statue of Mao Zedong graces the entrance to Tianfu Square, a vast pedestrian mall.

When the Bamboo Flowers...

The giant panda, one of the world's best-loved animals, has been known to science for little more than 100 years, yet it might vanish before another century passes. For the future of these furry black and white beasts is linked with the forests of bamboo that cover the mountains of southwest China, their only home.

The varieties of bamboo on which the panda feeds flower and then die off over vast areas, at intervals of decades, sometimes even a century. After this happens, it takes many months for the plants to grow again. Several hundred pandas died of starvation a few years ago when large tracts of bamboo flowered. There could be another bamboo famine soon, so Chinese and Western scientists are working on plans to save the pandas if that should happen.

Sixteen areas have been set aside as panda reserves; a research station is studying the movements and feeding habits of the animal; and Chengdu Zoo, which already breeds pandas, is geared to provide refuge and food for stricken creatures during a bamboo crisis. Today, there are thought to be only a thousand giant pandas left in the wild. No one knows how many will survive the next time the bamboo flowers.

By way of local colour, you shouldn't turn down a chance to see Sichuan opera. To make things more challenging, it's all sung in the local dialect, but you can just relax and watch the spectacle of mime, dance and acrobatics. Back-stage tours are arranged these days by private tour operators.

Chinese opera is characterised by mask-like make-up

Sichuan cuisine, one of the four great schools of Chinese cooking, produces such imaginative creations as abalone and chrysanthemums, peonies and butterflies and stewed bear paws in brown sauce. One of the most famous dishes, *mapo dofu*, consists of beancurd infused with chilli peppers in a manner that numbs the tongue on impact.

For the more adventurous, Chengdu is the gateway to the Great Buddha at Leshan, Mt Emei and the Daoist mountain of Qingchengshan. 100km (60 miles) northwest of Chengdu, the stunning Wolong Nature Reserve is an unspoilt region dedicated to the preservation and propagation of pandas. You may not actually spot any pandas in the wild unless you are very lucky, but they can be seen at the research centre.

CHONGQING (CHUNGKING)

Although the city's history goes back thousands of years, Chongqing was never a cultural centre, and it isn't today. It cannot offer spectacular temples, palaces or archaeological sites. Rather, it is a place to see the daily life of a major Chinese industrial city and to begin some outstanding excursions on the legendary Yangzi River.

In the Qin dynasty, in the 3rd century BC, the city was the capital of the dreamily named Kingdom of Ba. During the Tang

A ferry leaving Chongqing, on the muddy waters of the Yangzi

period (618–907) it was known as Yuzhou, and it is still called Yu for short. The emperor Zhao Dun, of the Song dynasty, renamed it Chongqing ('Twin Fortune') after two lucky events: he first became prince of the prefecture, then later emperor of China. Until the past few years it was spelled Chungking, by which name the city was best known in the West as the political and military capital of the nationalist government from 1939 to 1945, the wartime redoubt of Chiang Kai-shek. For several summers during the war, the town was bombed by the Japanese; but in the winters, enemy planes were prevented from doing any damage by the heavy fog that typically rises from the rivers, shrouding the town.

Although Chongqing is physically located in subtropical Sichuan (Szechuan) Province, since 1997 it has been an autonomous governmental municipality (as are Beijing, Shanghai and Tianjin), with a staggering metropolitan population of over 30 million people. Set on a promontory where the Yangzi and Jialing rivers converge, this starkly industrial city of smokestacks is crucial to transportation and commerce in southwest China.

It presides over the portion of the Yangzi upstream from the massive Three Gorges Dam project. In 1992, the National People's Congress passed a resolution to launch the ambitious Three Gorges Hydropower Project, including the construction of a huge dam and a reservoir, slated for completion some time after 2009 *(see pages 80 and 82)*.

Chongqing Sights

The sightseeing you remember best might be the lively free market lining the hundreds of steps that descend higgledy-piggledy from the hills of central Chongqing to the river. Bustling peasants hawk the rich harvest of the surrounding farming country: cabbages and oranges, eggs and live chickens (they are weighed while flapping), river fish and squirming eels, and table after table of the most fragrant spices, while stalls and hole-in-the-wall cafés heat up the city's number-one dish, the Sichuan hotpot.

At the tip of the peninsula where the two rivers meet is a small pavilion known as the **Gate to the Sky** (Chaotianmen), with a steep stone stairway leading down to the water's edge. The steps appear not to have been cleaned since the Ming dynasty, and are treacherously overlaid with mud and muck, so wear your safest shoes and walk with care. Fortunately, at the bottom of this long descent

Near the Chaotianmen pavilion, at the meeting of the two rivers, a mark indicates the level of the last great flood, in 1982, which covered a large area and caused great devastation.

there is a terminal for the funicular that returns you to the top of this town, which is so hilly that bicycles are almost unknown.

Sights worth seeing in town include the **Chongqing People's Hall**, built in 1953 to serve as a 4,000-seat conference hall and hotel. It blends the styles of the Ming and Qing dynasties with the needs of a modern conference hall. The **Chongqing Museum** (open daily 8.30am–5pm), while poorly lit and ageing, does contain a collection of dinosaur eggs and two 3,000-year-old wooden boats which, suspended from the cliffs of the Yangzi, served as caskets for nobles in the days of the Ba Kingdom. Perhaps the liveliest sight in Chongqing is the 1,000-year-old **Luohan Temple** (Luohansi; open daily 8.30am–5pm), where blind fortune-tellers and devoted followers of Buddha converge from dawn to dusk. Noted for 500 painted terracotta sculptures called *arhat*, the temple has recently been restored.

In the domain of darker political history, two former nationalist prisons outside town are open as monuments to the Revolutionary cause. The **Refuse Pit Prison** (Zhongmei Hezuosuo, also known as the US/Chiang Kai-shek Criminal Acts Exhibition Hall, open daily 8am–5pm), includes cells and torture chambers once used to jail suspected communists.

The **Bai Mansion** (Baigongguan; open daily 8am–5pm) is a smaller detention centre, with an equally dark past, found three kilometres (2 miles) down the hill.

Because of Chongqing's notoriously torrid summer weather – it's known as one of the 'furnaces' of China – hills and parks are a very welcome refuge here. **Loquat Hill** (Pipashan), the city's

A Controversial Dam

When it's fully operational in 2009, the Three Gorges Dam – 181m (594ft) high and 2,309m (7,575ft) long – will house 26 hydro turbine generators and will create a reservoir more than 660km (410 miles) long, stretching upriver to Chongqing. As well as controlling the Yangzi's devastating floods, it will provide electricity for central China. But although it will be a remarkable achievement, there are drawbacks – notably the forced relocation of more than 1.3 million local people, the loss of farmland and sites of historical interest, and the threat to rare species. The Yangzi river dolphin, Chinese alligator, Chinese sturgeon and Siberian crane may all suffer. There are worries, too, about the degenerating water quality in the reservoir, as much of the waste from settlements along the Yangzi is discharged directly into the river. And without constant dredging, the tons of sediments transported by the river may pose a threat to the dam's smooth operation.

During the rainy season, the Yangzi turns yellow with silt

highest spot, has gardens, a teahouse (Hongxing), and some splendid panoramas. The Northern and Southern Hot Springs parks (Beiwenquan and Nanwenquan) are also popular gathering places, with well-kept public gardens. During the years of Japanese air raids, hundreds of air-raid shelters were dug into the mountains here, and some have been turned into cafés and restaurants.

Even in the heat of summer, however, the most popular dish remains the Sichuan hotpot, a bowl of seething oils into which the diner dips and boils to perfection a selection of meats, vegetables and beancurd, much like fighting fire with fire. Chongqing's newest attraction is Ciqikou Old Town, a restored Ming Dynasty-era district of shops, cafés and teahouses.

Excursions from Chongqing

Yangzi River Cruise
Despite the impact of the dam project *(see box on page 80)*, China's most exciting boat trip remains the **Yangzi River cruise** through the spectacular **Three Gorges** (Sanxia). The most awe-

The Yangzi flows through majestic gorges

some scenery on the two-day stretch between Chongqing and Yichang is concentrated between the Sichuan city of **Baidi** and **Nanjin Pass** in Hubei Province. After the completion of the dam in 2009, the scenic beauty of the gorges will be diminished, but not destroyed.

Tourists can choose between ordinary Chinese passenger boats or more luxurious cruise ships that cater to overseas visitors. The river boats that the Chinese use lack frills, amenities and guides. The luxury craft charge much more but offer a good range of tourist services, including meals. Often reserved in part for package tours, these ships are also open to independent travellers, and staterooms can even be booked in advance from overseas with such lines as Victoria Cruises or Viking River Cruises.

For the latest information on the Three Gorges Hydropower Project, and its impact on cruises and the landscape, visitors considering taking the trip should contact their specialist travel agency or local operators such as CITS or China Highlights Travel (<www.chinahighlights.com/yangtzecruise>).

In June 2003 the Yangzi was blocked by the closure of 22 sluice gates, and the water in the reservoir behind was allowed to rise from 66m (215ft) to 135m (443ft). In May 2006 construction of the main wall of the dam was completed, and by 2009, when the dam becomes fully operational, the water level in the reservoir will have risen to 175m (574ft).

The Dazu Caves

One of China's great artistic wonders, rated on par with the Mogao Caves on the Silk Road in Dunhuang *(see page 93)*, is the Buddhist sculptural treasure of **Dazu** (open daily 8am–5pm). This district northwest of Chongqing was so inaccessible in earlier times that many thousands of statues were never exposed to pillage. Today, it still takes 2 hours to cover the 112km (70 miles) from Chongqing, even via the new Chengyu Expressway.

The stone carvings of Dazu were begun late in the 9th century during the Tang dynasty; the work lasted well into the Southern Song period, hundreds of years later. Although Buddhism is their central theme, there are also sculptures representing historical and human-interest subjects.

Northern Hill (Beishan), situated only a couple of kilometres north of Dazu, begins with a Buddhist temple and a big, animated square. The wide, rocky valley below is filled with sculpture; every inch of stone seems to have been carved. Among the perfectly preserved figures in 'The Wheel of the Universe' in Grotto 136 are the statues of two holy women, the bodhisattvas Manjusri and Samatabhadra, who triumphed over evil. Helping to make Northern Hill an overwhelming experience is the presence of Buddhist pilgrims who still call upon these ancient shrines.

Even more magnificent is **Treasure Peak** (Baodingshan). Its sculptures are located in a natural arc of stone known as the Great Buddha Crescent, carved over a 70-year span by Buddhist monks during the Southern Song dynasty (1127–1279). The biggest single work, an immense reclining Buddha 29m (96ft)

Dazu's huge Reclining Buddha, surrounded by disciples

long, is surrounded by the infinitely smaller statues of lifelike disciples. Whereas grotto sculpture in China is usually laid out more or less spontaneously, the caves here were apparently all planned to the last detail before the first stone was chipped, thus eliminating any repetition. Dazu represents the last great period of Buddhist cave sculpture in China, and a long day's journey out and back from Chongqing to this stone crescent is unforgettable.

DALI

In Yunnan Province, about 250km (155 miles) northwest of its capital Kunming along the historic Burma Road route, is the scenic village of **Dali**, a favourite destination for independent backpackers. The surroundings could hardly be more spectacular, with Erhai ('Ear Sea') Lake to the east and the steep Cangshan mountain range to the west. Best of all are the people of Dali, who are mostly members of the Bai branch of the Yi minority, outgoing people who treat Western travellers with wonderful hospitality.

The town, capital of the Bai Autonomous Region, has sections of a medieval wall with formal gates on the north and south ends. Within the walls are a few intersecting main streets whose tile-roofed shops and houses now serve as souvenir shops, private travel agencies, hostels, and – above all – small, intimate, friendly cafés serving a truly international mix of inexpensive dishes.

The café life in Dali is one of its chief delights. Cafés are perfect spots to wile away the hours over coffee or beer or to meet local Bai people as well as other travellers. Perhaps the most famous of the dozens of cafés is Mr China Son's Cultural Exchange Café, run by Uncle Li (Heliyi), the first Bai in history to go abroad. His autobiography, on sale at his café, is an epic soap opera.

Dali Sights

Dali also has sights and attractions well worth attending to when the café and bistro scene begins to pale. **Erhai Lake**, the second largest in Yunnan, is a 30-minute walk from town, and its main village, Caicun, is a maze of unpaved alleys and mud houses. Ferries cross the lake to even more remote villages, including the temple dedicated to Guanyin (goddess of mercy) on **Putuo Island**. Any of dozens of local travel agents can quickly arrange an excursion to lakeside villages, including the market at **Wase**. One popular diversion is the Monday morning outdoor market at **Shaping**, 30 minutes up the eucalyptus-lined road by minibus from Dali. It's a vast market of country wares, batik and horse-trading, with hundreds of locals dressed in their traditional bright Bai jackets, tunics and plumed caps.

The chief monument at Dali is the **Temple of the Three Pagodas** (Santasi; open daily 8am–7pm), founded in 825. The towering structures (all sealed up) are in the close-eaves style that set the pattern for later pagodas in the province. The tallest, and oldest, of the three rises to 16 tiers and 70m (230ft). The pagodas have survived several earthquakes, though the original temple has not. Excavations during a 1979 renovation unearthed a trove of exquisite artefacts – gold Buddhas, silver pheonixes, bronze

Bai women sell their wares at Shaping's outdoor market

mirrors and copper utensils. The complex is ringed by hundreds of stalls, many of them selling specimens of the local marble.

There are also temples and pagodas in the steep foothills of the Cangshan (Green Mountain) range. Although seldom open, they provide the perfect ornaments for a day's hike from vista to vista over this long, narrow valley that reaches west to Tibet.

While young adventurous travellers still flock to Dali, the opening of several new hotels and a modern airport an hour away have brought this exquisite little Chinese Shangri-La within the reach of many more visitors.

As Dali attracts more and more tourists, travellers are heading out into even more remote regions of northwestern Yunnan. The village of **Lijiang**, 150km (95 miles) north of Dali, is gorgeous. Rising up outside town is the dramatic 5,500-m (18,000-ft) Jade Dragon Snow Mountain (Yulongxue Shan), which you can ascend by cable car to a considerable altitude. The old part of Lijiang – cut with waterways, decorated with attractive local

The old town of Lijiang, reconstructed after an earthquake in 1996

architecture and populated with blue-clothed members of the Naxi minority – is even quainter than Dali, despite the intrusion of commercialisation and growing numbers of tourists (thanks to the airport). This antique village in the heart of the city was designated a World Heritage Site by UNESCO in 1999, three years after a severe earthquake nearly destroyed it.

At the north end of town in Black Dragon Pool Park, the **Naxia Dongbei Cultural Museum** (open daily 8.30am–6pm) is devoted to minorities. A variety of evening musical performances are held in Lijiang by Naxi musicians and dancers, with the most famous being staged nightly by the Naxi Orchestra.

Lijiang is also the jumping off point for the popular two- to three-day hike along the stunning 30-km (18-mile) long **Tiger Leaping Gorge** (Hutiaoxia). The hike can be dangerous in parts, depending on the weather, so enquire in Lijiang about conditions along the gorge before setting out.

DATONG

It takes about 7 hours by train from Beijing to reach Datong, to the west of the capital in Shanxi Province. Datong itself is a rather poor coal-mining and industrial city set on a plateau 1,000m (3,250ft) above sea level. The summers are short here on the edge of Inner Mongolia, and winters are glacial. It's not the sort of place poets would eulogise, yet for nearly a century (398–494) it served as the capital of the Northern Wei dynasty.

Three monasteries and a famous dragon screen recall Datong's once stately history. The **Nine Dragon Wall** (Jiulongbi; open daily 8am–6pm in summer, 9am–5pm in winter), a Ming landmark (1392), stands in the old part of town among the narrow streets lined by single-storey houses. This is said to be the largest and oldest screen of its type anywhere in China, at 457m (1,500ft) certainly longer than the more famous version in the Forbidden City. The ceramic mural shows nine dragons, each in a different dynamic pose. When the sun reflects on the pool that runs along the base of the wall, the glazed tile figures flash to life.

The **Huayan Monastery** (Hwayansi; open daily 8am–6pm in summer, 9am–5pm in winter), built under the Liao dynasty in the 11th century, was finished by the Jin dynasty rulers in 1140. The monastery is unusual in that it faces east and not, as was customary in China, south. The main building, the Great Treasure Hall (Daxiongbaodian), is one of the two biggest Buddhist halls still standing in China. The fine ceiling comprises 749 illustrated squares, no two the same. In the centre are enthroned the Five Buddhas of the Five Directions, relics of the Ming dynasty.

The other big temple in town, **Shanhua Monastery** (Shanhuasi; open daily 8am–6pm), faces the old city wall, which is undergoing renovation. The monastery dates from 713, in the Tang dynasty, but it was largely rebuilt after a 12th-century fire. Standing in the grand, red-walled pavilion are 24 celestial guardians, each of distinct mien. A circular 'moon gate' in the side wall of the monastery leads to the Five Dragon Wall (Wulongbi), transplanted here from a former Confucian temple. This ceramic screen resembles the lavish Nine Dragon Wall in the town centre, but here the middle dragon, terrifyingly, faces forward.

> **Though Xuankongsi is a Daoist temple, in its Three Religions Hall Buddha, Confucius and Lao Tse sit side by side.**

A major attraction near Datong is the **Temple Suspended Over the Void** (Xuankongsi; open daily 9am–5pm), situated a 2-hour car journey south through a barren sandstone plateau. Tours usually stop along the way at one of the area's cave houses, where residents are happy to show off their hand-dug quarters. The 6th-century temple is spectacular, with over 40 halls and pavilions suspended as if by magic on the face of a sheer limestone cliff – some of the rooms supported by only a single pillar – and connected to each other by ornate catwalks. Signs indicate the safe route for visitors to wind up, down and around to reach over 80 statues of Buddha and other treasures.

This giant seated Buddha dominates No. 20 of the Yungang Caves

The Yungang Caves

Most tourists head for Datong in pursuit of history and art, and they are not disappointed. The city is best known for the **Yungang Caves** (Yungang Shiku; open daily 8.30am–5.30pm), which are 16km (10 miles) west of Datong and contain one of China's most treasured displays of ancient Buddhist sculpture. When the pious project was ordered by the Northern Wei rules to atone for their earlier persecution of Buddhism, some 30,000 artisan families from Dunhuang were forcibly relocated to work on the caves. Thousands of sculptors took 50 years to create about 100,000 statues, carved into the walls of the 20 rock temples. About 50,000 statues remain – from the size of a postage stamp to the height of a five-storey house – despite the rigours of time, weather and marauders. The sculptural style was mainly borrowed from Indian Buddhist art, which itself grew from a synthesis of various foreign styles, including Persian, Byzantine and even Greek.

After running the gauntlet of souvenir shops and stalls, visitors enter the caves through a monastery where 2,000 monks once lived. A wooden structure four storeys high, built in the Ming dynasty, blocks the winds that blast the caves. Carvings of the fanciful Third Son of the Dragon protect the building from fire. Tours usually begin at Cave No. 5, which contains a seated Buddha figure 17m (56ft) high. The gold plating, an after-thought, was added in the Qing dynasty. As in most of the caves, the walls are filled with niches and small statues. In Cave No. 6, nearly square in plan, a pagoda reaches to the ceiling. The life of the Buddha from birth to the attainment of nirvana is illustrated in an intricately carved frieze running around the pagoda walls and the sides of the cave. The decoration in this cave is consid-ered the supreme achievement of Yungang.

Cave No. 7 is notable for its beautifully carved ceiling. At the entrance to No. 8, graceful Indian-style statues face each other. No. 9 contains the smallest of all Buddha figures here, only 2cm (less than 1in) high. In Cave No. 10, note the Greek influ-ence in the headdress of the guardian figure carved at the entrance. Cave No. 11 is said to contain some 12,000 Buddha figures, more than any other cave; high up on the wall is a tablet reporting that 83 artists worked for six years to complete the carvings in this one grotto. In No. 12, heavenly musicians carved over the entrance are playing 12 different ancient instru-ments. Notice an unusual feature of the giant statue in No. 13: the Buddha's right wrist is supported by the small figure of a four-armed sportsman.

Cave No. 14 has suffered severe damage. (In general the wind has eroded the outward-facing walls in most of the caves; the best-preserved carvings tend to be on the opposite walls.) The Cave of Ten Thousand Buddhas is No. 15; the figures in this cave are arranged in a pigeon-hole grid pattern.

The oldest caves of the whole complex – dating from the 5th century – are numbered 16 to 20. (The currently used east-to-west numbering scheme was inaugurated in modern times and bears little resemblance to the system used in earlier centuries.) In Cave No. 16 are three holes pierced through the outer wall, showing the original positions of three Buddhas appropriated by foreign collectors; tour guides here say they are now in New York's Metropolitan Museum. Cave No. 17, like its neighbours on either side, has an oval floor-plan. The Buddha's upper arms sport Greek-style armbands.

The giant standing Buddha in Cave No. 18 wears a strange vestment called the 'Thousand Buddha Robe'; on the front of the garment the sculptor has carved a throng of mini-Buddha figures. Cave No. 20, the last one carved while Datong was the capital of the Northern Wei dynasty, is occupied by a giant seated Buddha. It's all the more dramatic since the front wall has crumbled away, leaving the statue open to the sky.

DUNHUANG

It used to take 24 hours by train, plus a cruel 2–3-hour bus or jeep journey, to reach the sleepy desert town of Dunhuang, in Gansu province. Now it's an easy plane ride from Xi'an or Beijing. Dun-

Two stupas near Dunhuang, on the edge of the Western Desert

Mogao was a major Buddhist centre on the Silk Road

huang has come a long way since the days when the Silk Road camel trains stopped here. Camels still work in and around Dunhuang, pulling ploughs or transporting cargo. If you've just come from over-populated eastern China, you might feel all but alone in a town of only 10,000. Although some donkey carts and bicycles occasionally impinge on the tranquillity of the main street, the townsfolk have plenty of time to stand around and gossip.

In China even provincial museums can be treasure troves. The **Dunhuang County Museum** (Dunhuang Bowuguan; open daily 8am–6.30pm) in the centre of town overflows with Silk Road relics, from works of art to 2,000-year-old chopsticks. The first hall is devoted to calligraphic rarities found in Cave No. 17 of the Mogao Caves. Paper documents have survived for 1,000 years in the dry climate of the cave. In the second room, sacrificial objects unearthed in ancient tombs are shown alongside pots, a plough and armour. Ancient handicrafts displayed in the third hall include a Tang dynasty chess set, a present from the governor to the emperor. At the edge of town stands the **White Horse Dagoba** (Baima Tai; open daily 9am–6pm), reminiscent of Beijing's White Dagoba. This is where the white horse of the famous travelling Indian monk Kumarajiva (344–413) is said to have died.

The Mogao Caves

In spite of the difficulties, tourists still head for this 2,000-year-old town to see China's most magnificent ancient murals and painted statues. They're certainly worth another 25km (15 miles).

➤   The **Mogao Caves** (open daily 8.30am–5pm), hewn from a desert cliffside, tell the story of the great flowering of Buddhist art in China. They were created in fits and starts over 1,000 years: the first caves are said to have been built by the monk Lezun in 366AD, the last ones carved out at the time of the Mongolian conquest in 1277. After that, Mogao sank into oblivion, until the monk Wang Yuanlu settled here at the beginning of the 20th century. The first cave he opened is the one now numbered 16. In the adjacent cave, No. 17, he found more than 4,000 manuscripts.

Statistics aren't everything, but consider that there are 45,000 sq m (484,000 sq ft) of mural paintings. They cover the walls and ceilings with brightly coloured pictures of men and gods and speculations about eternity. The clay of Mogao, unlike the cliff boulders of grottoes further east, is ill-suited to large carvings, so artists created stucco figurines and frescoes. And in the

---

The Strict Rules of the Caves

A notice at the entrance of the Mogao Caves lists all the things you may not do. It is forbidden to sit down or to lean on the barriers, and to carry bags, cameras, hats or sticks, for fear that these might scrape against the murals. And children shorter than 1.4m (4ft 7in) are not allowed in the caves. Although around 40 of the grottoes are open to the public, you can only see them on a guided tour, which will visit a dozen or so (different caves on different days).

The murals have survived for over 1,000 years thanks to the desert climate and the pigments used – and the fact that they have not been exposed to the light. For this reason, they are not permanently illuminated today, and flash photography is strictly prohibited. Your guide will shine his flashlight on to selected frescoes, adding a hint of archaeological adventure to the proceedings, and you may also use your own torch – briefly – to examine features in detail. Postcards, slides and picture books, as well as copies of the wall paintings produced by local artists, are on sale in a shop on the site.

same caves stand more than 2,000 painted sculptures, realistic or fantastical. Of the several hundred grottoes still intact, only a few dozen are open to the public. And even these are kept locked so that visits can be supervised. The outer walls of the caves have been reinforced, with walkways added. Tours cover various itineraries. Here are some highlights:

Northern Wei dynasty (386–534). Statues with Persian or Indian faces. Graceful, life-like animal paintings with three-dimensional effects.

Sui dynasty (581–618). Illustrations of religious stories. Notice the emotions revealed in the characters' faces; also, Chinese robes have replaced foreign dress.

Tang dynasty (618–907). Don't miss Cave No. 96, a nine-tiered temple from the 7th century. The seated Buddha statue inside has toes as long as your arm. Cave No. 158 is filled with a statue of the reclining Buddha, the face particularly peaceful and godly when seen from the far left. You'll be struck by the imagination, life and colour of the Tang wall paintings.

Later dynasties. Murals from the 10th century onwards provide valuable details of everyday life in medieval China.

Crescent Moon Lake

Most of the desert is grey and menacing, a sea of gravel out of which stark rocky mountains occasionally appear. But everybody's dream desert can be seen a few kilometres south of Dunhuang. With oases in sight, awesome dunes rise in waves to 250-m (800-ft) crests. As the sun and clouds move, the colours and textures of the sand hills change.

Hidden between the hills is a small, clear lake – **Crescent Moon Lake** (Yueyahu). It's not a mirage. Reeds grow at the edge of this cool blue spring and tiny fish swim in it. You can reach the lake from the edge of the desert on the back of a camel or (if you like walking in sand) on foot. Twenty minutes each way should do it. Beside the pool is a magnificent pavilion tower with a teahouse. For a rare desert experience, climb to the top of a dune and listen to the musical – or thunderous – sound as the sand slides down. This is the same sound that Marco Polo heard when he passed this way on his own camel caravan 700 years ago.

GUANGZHOU (CANTON)

Foreigners have been turning up in Guangzhou for a couple of thousand years, for it was China's first major seaport. It was the first Chinese town to receive Europeans, when a Portuguese flotilla arrived in 1514. All this has made for such dramatic historical incidents as the Opium Wars, which broke out when the authorities cracked down on the opium trade here. This crowded city has maintained its gateway role. Ever since 1957, the biannual Canton Trade Fair (now the Guangzhou Trade Fair) has attracted throngs of international business people. Even in the years of political upheaval, Guangzhou kept open the nation's ties with foreign countries and with overseas Chinese, millions of whom have their roots here in Guangdong Province.

Guangzhou is one of China's most affluent cities

Guangzhou straddles the **Pearl River** (Zhu Jiang), China's fifth-longest river, which links the metropolis to the South China Sea. The waterway provides a good deal of charm and excitement. The daily drama of ferryboats, freighters, junks with dirty grey sails, low-lying sampans – even small tankers and big

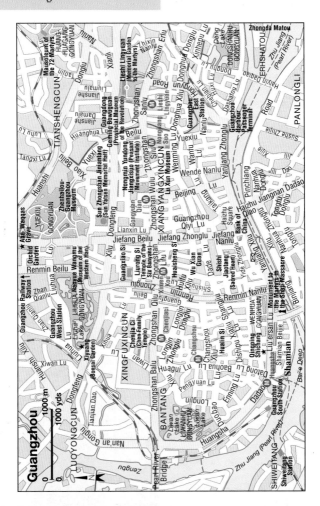

gunboats – unfolds right in the centre of town. The river is also used to irrigate the surrounding farmlands, which yield a cornucopia of rice, fruit and vegetables.

With a population more than 7 million, Guangzhou is primarily an industrial city and has more than 3,200 factories. Production lines turn out buses, ships, agricultural machinery, chemicals and sewing machines. It is one of China's richest cities, with new skyscrapers, motorways, two metro lines and fashionable shopping centres to prove it. Although the economy has changed radically in recent years, many local traditions live on, including the love of flowers, Cantonese Opera and the local dialect (incomprehensible to fellow Chinese). And then there is Cantonese food – some say the world's greatest cuisine – much appreciated in its adaptations internationally but unrivalled when created in its home kitchen.

Guangzhou in History

In the 3rd century BC the founder of the Qin dynasty annexed the remote Guangzhou area, thus furnishing China with its first major seaport. By the end of the Han dynasty, foreign trade linked the port with other areas of Asia as well as with the Roman Empire. The name Guangzhou was bestowed during the Kingdom of Wu (3rd century AD), but foreigners came to call it 'Canton'.

As commerce expanded, so did the foreign population of the port: by the 9th century, large colonies of Arabs, Jews, Persians and others had settled here. They traded in tea, silk and porcelain, all commodites that were in constant demand abroad. It was to be another seven centuries before Europeans established themselves in Canton. The Portuguese were first, followed by Spaniards, Dutch and British. The Chinese authorities tried to keep the foreigners at arm's length, limiting their activities to certain districts and seasons.

The expansion of trade did eventually bring conflict, because China would accept nothing less than silver bullion in payment for its exports. However, the wily British soon thought of an alternative commodity: opium *(see pages 35–6)*.

The Opium Wars ended in 1842 with the Treaty of Nanking (later denounced as 'unequal'). Under the terms of the treaty, China was compelled to open 'Canton' and four other ports to foreign penetration.

When the ever shakier Qing dynasty fell in 1911, Guangzhou became the centre of the republican movement founded by Guangdong's most famous son, Dr Sun Yat-sen, and the head-quarters of the Guomindang (Nationalists), the first modern political party in China. The modernisation of Guangzhou began in the early 1920s; what remained of the old city wall was pulled down and most of the main streets that define the city today were built in a frenzied 18 months of construction. In 1927, the troops of Chiang Kai-shek wiped out the com-munist-led forces who had established the Guangzhou Commune. During World War II the Japanese occupied the city. In the subsequent civil war, Guangzhou briefly served as the nationalist capital before the communists captured the city and gained power nationwide in 1949.

> **During a period of cooperation between the Guomindang and the communists, Mao Zedong taught at Guangzhou's Institute of Peasant Movements, and Zhou Enlai at the military academy.**

Monuments and Parks

Guangzhou can't claim to compete with Beijing or Xi'an when it comes to sightseeing attractions. But its monuments and parks are well worth visiting, not least for the chance to mingle with the Cantonese people themselves. **Yue Xiu Park** (open daily 6am–9pm), near the Trade Fair in the northern part of the city, covers a 93-hectare (230-acre) site. In addition to its pretty gar-dens, lakes, pavilions and sports facilities, Guangzhou's largest park also contains the city's oldest building, the red 'Tower Overlooking the Sea' (Zhenhailou). 'Tower' is a misleading description for this building of five storeys. Built in 1380, it now houses the **Guangzhou Museum** (Guangzhou Bowuguan; open daily 9am–5.30pm). With signs in English and Chinese, the museum is quite interesting and includes artefacts and displays recording the city's contacts with the West (from Bibles to radios), and the extraordinary journeys of the imperial eunuch Zheng He who, between 1405 and 1433, travelled as far as East Africa, the Persian Gulf and Java. The top floor of this watch-tower museum is now a charming teahouse.

Another equally famous modern landmark in the park is the **Statue of the Five Rams** (Wu Yang Shixiang), a granite sculptural representation of five handsome beasts, based on the legend of Guangzhou's founding. It is said that five gods descended from heaven riding rams holding sprigs of rice in their mouths. The celestial visitors distributed the rice, blessing the local people with eternal freedom from famine. The gods then disappeared, according to the story, but the five rice-bearing rams turned to stone. And here they are (or at least their replicas), giving Guangzhou its nickname: 'City of Rams'.

The Sun Yat-sen Memorial Hall can seat 5,000

In the northwest corner of the park, the **Orchid Garden** (Lan Pu; open daily 8am–9pm) is filled with more than 10,000 pots and 200 varieties of orchids.

Near the park entrance is the new **Nan Yue Museum** (open daily 9am–5pm), which displays the contents of the adjacent Tomb of the Southern Yue Kings, who ruled southern China in the second century BC.

Dr Sun Yat-sen (1866–1925), who began his political career in the city, is honoured in Yuexiu Park by an obelisk 30m (100ft) tall. South of the park is an even more impressive monument, the **Sun Yat-sen Memorial Hall**, built in 1931. This vast, modern version of a traditional Chinese building, with its sweeping blue-tile roofs, contains an auditorium big enough to seat nearly 5,000.

Guangzhou's principal Buddhist monument, the **Temple of the Six Banyan Trees** (Liurongsi; open daily 8am–5.30pm), was founded over 1,400 years ago. The trees that inspired the 11th-century poet and calligrapher Su Dongpo to name the temple have since died, but the often-restored complex remains a focus of local Buddhist activities. Overlooking it all is the **Flower Pagoda** (Huata), a slender relic of the Song dynasty. From the outside, the pagoda appears to be just nine tiers high, but there are actually 17 floors inside. Adjacent is an unusual 'death hall', where the departed (their pictures posted on the walls) are remembered in daily prayers – for a fee, of course.

A typical European-style 19th-century building on Shamian

In the early medieval period, Guangzhou had a significant Muslim population as a result of trade with the Middle East. The city is home to the oldest mosque in China, the **Huaisheng Mosque** (open daily 6am–5pm), built in 627 and rebuilt several times since. Its white minaret can be climbed via a spiral staircase for a view of the courtyards, gardens and Guangzhou's modern skyscrapers, but sometimes access to the mosque is not allowed.

> The Huaisheng Mosque is said to have been founded by a trader who was an uncle of the Prophet Mohammed. Arab traders did visit China in the 7th century, so the story may be true.

The city's leading tribute to the days of imperial splendour is the **Chen Family Temple** (Chenjiaci; open daily 8.30am–5.30pm), a memorial to members of a large merchant clan from all over China. This sprawling compound of courtyards, shops, a museum and showy 19th-century pavilions is decorated in a pantheon of finely carved friezes, gates and gold-leaf tableaux depicting scenes of Chinese myth and romance.

Shamian Island

The atmosphere of 19th-century colonial 'Canton' is best evoked by **Shamian Island**, in the Pearl River, linked to central Guangzhou by several bridges. This small residential enclave, shaded by banyan trees, was the closed community of the foreign colony in the era of the Western 'concessions'. The stately European-style buildings, including old banks, factories and churches, have been spruced up, and Shamian's wide, shaded streets are free from the incessant traffic that plagues the rest of the city. Pavement cafés, boutiques, traditional craft shops and the impressive White Swan Hotel make this Guangzhou's leading place for a stroll.

Across from Shamian Island is China's most notorious and colourful marketplace, **Qingping** (open daily 8am–6pm). A maze of alleys crammed with 2,000 stalls, Qingping offers up acres of herbs, spices, jade, antiques, memorabilia, goldfish, songbirds and a sometimes nightmarish display of live animals destined for the kitchen, including dogs, cats and rare species.

Among modern attractions, the flashiest is **Oriental Studio 2000** (open daily 9am–5pm), Guangzhou's answer to Hollywood's Universal City, where daily shows are staged on two movie sets, one evoking Shanghai in the 1930s, the other a traditional courtyard in the throes of a kung fu battle.

No visit to Guangzhou is complete without indulging in its famous cuisine, particularly its fresh seafood and delicate dim sum. Two of the best dining spots are its traditional garden restaurants, Beiyuan and Banxi. Beiyuan, famous for its dim sum, consists of over 40 dining pavilions and tearooms, each decorated in intricate latticework. Banxi, on the shores of Liwan Lake, also has a classic

decor, with etched glass from the Qing dynasty and delicacies to match. The availability and proximity of fresh ingredients is one good reason why Cantonese food tastes so special in its native city.

GUILIN

China's most famous landscapes, the subjects of thousands of paintings, are to be found in Guilin. The 'finest mountains and rivers under heaven' are so inspiring that poets, artists and tourists have made this China's number one natural attraction. The climate is subtropical, with an annual rainfall of 190cm (75in), so avoid the rainiest season, from April through to July. An additional incentive

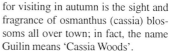

for visiting in autumn is the sight and fragrance of osmanthus (cassia) blossoms all over town; in fact, the name Guilin means 'Cassia Woods'.

Tourists are so numerous in the otherwise relaxed shopping district of Guilin that the pedestrian crossings have signs in English as well as Chinese. Another cosmopolitan influence comes from the area's many minority peoples: Guilin is part of the Guangxi-Zhuang Autonomous Region, which borders Vietnam. The proliferation of so-called Muslim restaurants is explained by the presence here of thousands of people of the traditionally Muslim Zhuang nationality, China's largest minority group.

The geological history of Guilin, the key to the wonder of its moody

The sun rises over the Li River and its dramatic limestone spires

mountains and caves, goes back several hundred million years. The area was under the sea when an upheaval raised it to the status of terra firma. Later it was flooded, then lifted again in further cataclysmic events. The alternation of sea water and air through the millennia created limestone formations called karst, which eroded into pinnacles, mounds and peaks that captivate the imagination.

Guilin was settled more than 2,000 years ago when the Ling Canal was built, effectively linking the great Yangzi and Pearl rivers. The Ling Canal, one of the world's longest, still exists and can be easily seen at Xi'ang, 65km (40 miles) northwest of here. Guilin's connection with one of mankind's most ambitious engineering projects was important, but otherwise little was heard from the town. It served as provincial capital for several hundred years, and in modern times, thanks to the profusion of caves to hide in, was a centre for resistance during the war with Japan – and as a result Guilin was razed by the Japanese army in

Reed Flute Cave is full of bizarre stalactites and stalagmites

1944. Today, rebuilt from the rubble of war, the city is thriving, thanks in large measure to its spectacular scenery and the tourists it attracts. Guilin's best shops and restaurants are located downtown in the new **Central Square**, especially along Yiren Lu and the pedestrianised street, Zhengyang Buxing Jie.

Limestone Pinnacles

The best way to appreciate Guilin's unique setting is to climb to the summit of one of its limestone pinnacles: for example, 150-m (640-ft) Solitary Beauty Peak (Duxiu Feng) near the centre of town, or the hill called Diecaishan, to the north. The latter name means 'Piled Silk Hill', or 'Folded Brocade Hill', a metaphor suggested by the layers of rock. Hiking to the look-out point at the top is strenuous, but catching your breath is only one of the good reasons for stopping along the way. For instance, there's Breezy Cave, which cuts through the hill from south to north. It is permanently cooled by a refreshing breeze, to the relief of crowds on hot summer days. The many inscriptions carved into the cave walls over the centuries are much admired by connoisseurs of calligraphy.

At the summit, where the altitude is 223m (732ft), the charmingly named **Catch-Cloud Pavilion** (Nayunting) provides a 360-degree panorama. The view is worth savouring: the winding river, the tile-roofed cityscape, the green flat farmland and the mist-shrouded hills fading into the distance.

Elephant Trunk Park (Xiangshan Gongyuan; open daily 6.30am–11.30pm) features Guilin's most famous peak, **Elephant Trunk Hill** (Xiangbi Shan). The leafy limestone pachyderm stands at the meeting point of the Li River and the Peach Blossom River. On top of the peak stands the **Puxian Pagoda**, built during the Song dynasty as an offering to calm the flood-prone river. The hill is illuminated at night.

So too is **Fuboshan** ('Whirlpool Hill'), another natural stone tower closer to the city centre, with a view as well as other distractions. According to legend, a General Fubo, who passed this way 2,000 years ago, tested his sword in the Sword-Testing Stone, a stalactite formation that comes down to within inches

Today fishing with cormorants on the Li is done mostly for tourists

of the ground. Further on, the Thousand Buddha Cliff is carved with several hundred figures dating from the Tang and Song dynasties.

The **District of the Two Lakes**, in the southern part of town, has been made into a delightful public park with gardens, walkways and pagodas. Originally, Banyan Tree Lake (Ronghu) and Fir Tree Lake (Shahu) were a single expanse, forming part of the moat which protected the city wall. The Song dynasty-era Green Belt Bridge across the middle created the two lakes.

Reed Flute Cave (Ludiyan; open daily 8.30–11am and 12.30–3.30pm) takes its name from the reeds – which were used to make flutes – that once grew at its entrance. Today the entry is marked by a ticket booth, where guides meet visitors to take them on an illuminated tour 500m into the mountain's interior. As in most other caverns, certain formations have been given poetic names. The cave's largest chamber, called the Crystal Palace of the Dragon King, can accommodate 1,000 people, and was where many local citizens sheltered during the Japanese bombing campaign.

On the eastern bank of the Li lies **Seven Star Park** (Qixing Gongyuan; open daily 7am–9.30pm). It acquired its name from the position of its seven hills, which suggest the pattern of the Plough (Big Dipper) constellation. In the centre of the park rises Camel Hill (Luotou Shan), which indeed does uncannily resemble a camel. Another attraction is the **Forest of Steles**, a cliff where poems and pictures have been carved into the rock over the past 1,500 years.

But the true star of Seven Star Park is **Seven Star Cave** (Qixing Dong) – a mere million years old and a tourist attraction for more than 1,000 years. Some of the scenic formations of stalactites and stalagmites have names like Old Banyan Tree Welcoming Guests and Dragon Splashing Water, providing an idea of the poetic licence enjoyed by Chinese cave explorers. The round-trip tour of this cave is considerably longer than the itinerary in the Reed Flute Cave. Both underworlds have constant, comfortable temperatures year-round, but they are dripping with a humidity that makes the going slippery.

One of Guilin's newer attractions is the **Minorities Cultural Park** (Minsu Fengqingyuan; open daily 8.30am–11pm), on the eastern shore of the Li River. In this ethnic amusement park, members of the Zhuang, Dong and Miao minorities display their native cultures while dressed in traditional costume.

Li River Boat Trip

The transcendent tourist experience of Guilin is a boat trip on the **Li River**. The limestone scenery could hardly be more romantic. But life along the river is also quite fascinating: washerwomen squatting on the shore, water buffalo ambling down for a dip, the improvised ferryboats, and the captive cormorant birds, their necks ringed to prevent them from swallowing all their catch, waiting for orders to go fishing from bamboo rafts.

Large, flat-bottomed tour boats usually leave early in the morning from the quay near the Liberation Bridge in central Guilin. (In the dry season, when the river is at its lowest, the first part of the journey is by coach.) With room for more than 100 passengers each, most of these vessels are quiet and serve a lunch cooked en route. The river traffic, meanwhile, keeps amateur photographers snapping in all directions at flat-bottomed tubs, hand-poled bamboo rafts, sampans and towboats.

Images unroll before the eye like a painted scroll as your boat continues downstream: Tunnelled Hill, Pagoda Hill (also known as Battleship Hill), Washing Vase Hill and Fighting Cocks Hills (facing each other across the river). A large village on the left bank, **Dragon Gate Village**, is noted for water chestnuts and its 1,000-year-old banyan tree.

To the south is a much larger village, **Daxu**, with a high bridge from the Ming period called 'Longevity Bridge'. Here and elsewhere, the rich, flat land produces the ingredients for a formidable fruit salad: oranges and grapefruit, chestnuts and persimmons, plus exotic tropical delicacies all but unknown outside Asia. Adding to the entrancing beauty of the scene, great stands of a feathery variety of bamboo grow along the riverbanks, forming huge cascades of green.

Beyond the village of Yangdi unfolds the uncanny scenery that prompted a Chinese poet more than 1,000 years ago to write: 'The river is a green silk belt, the mountains emerald hairpins'. Peaks and pinnacles crowd the river, white goats cling to steep mountainsides, and an eagle soars high above the cliffs. The river itself flows green and transparent. Credit for this limpid rarity goes not only to the strict anti-pollution standards to protect the River Li but also to nature itself, which endows the water with a high content of carbonic acid.

Mural Hill is so called because the sheer cliff face comprises so many patches of colour that it might be a fresco. In the lights and shadows of the cliff, the shapes of nine different horses can be discerned, hence the cliff's alternative name, 'Nine Horse Hill' (Jiumahuashan). Near the end of the voyage, the village of Xingping comes into view on the left bank, surrounded by magical scenery – landmarks with names like Snail Hill and Five Fingers Hill.

The boat trip ends at the county town of **Yangshuo**, which is romantically set among stunning limestone pinnacles and a highly popular destination. The scenery around Yangshuo is even prettier than Guilin and, without the full-on tour-group tourism of Guilin, attracts droves of independent travellers. In Yangshuo, the eerie landscapes are closer at hand, and there are superb views from the hilltop pavilion in the city park, from the

View from Moon Hill, near Yangshuo

port and from the bridge to the south. The local economy is largely propped up by the numerous cafés and bars that stretch along Xi Jie, which is where you will also find travel agencies and tour guides. Many travellers jump on bicycles (available to hire everywhere) and head out of town. Perhaps the best trip is to **Moon Hill** (Yueliang Shan), 50 minutes outside town by bike. Make your way to the top (while fending off insistent hawkers and postcard sellers) for unparalleled views of the Yangshuo countryside. Other popular activities in Yangshuo include rock-climbing, trips up the River Li and cave exploration.

The 83-km (52-mile) cruise on the Li takes only 4–5 hours, but there is no river trip like it. The trip back to Guilin by minibus provides yet another facet of the soaring scenery.

HANGZHOU

Several dozen lakes in China are named 'West Lake', but only one is so celebrated that it needs no further identification. It is West Lake (Xihu) in Hangzhou, on China's east coast. The Song dynasty poet

Su Dongpo likened West Lake to one of ancient China's greatest beauties, Xizi – who was also calm, soft, delicate and enchanting. (The girls of Hangzhou are still famous for their light, clear complexion, which is attributed to the mild, humid climate.)

But Hangzhou has more than scenery. The capital of Zhejiang Province, one of the most prosperous regions in China, Hangzhou is 189km (117 miles) from Shanghai – about 3 hours by train and 2 hours by bus or car on the new toll road. A city of over a million people, rich in historic and cultural monuments, it also offers some educational outings. Here you can see how two of China's major inventions, silk and tea, are produced. Hangzhou's pharmaceutical industry and academy of arts are well-known throughout China.

Historically, Hangzhou enjoyed 237 years of imperial glory from the 9th century onward. In 1138 the newly formed Southern Song dynasty took Hangzhou as its temporary residence. The town flourished, with officials, writers and scholars moving here as the dynasty blossomed. In all, 14 kings and emperors held court here.

Countless boats continually criss-cross West Lake

When Marco Polo visited in the 13th century, he pronounced the city superior to 'all others in the world, in grandeur and beauty as well as its abundant delights, which might lead an inhabitant to imagine himself in paradise'. Hangzhou is the southern terminus of the world's first great canal, the **Grand Canal**, which is still in use. It is said that the emperor extended it to Hangzhou so that he could choose concubines from among the city's most beautiful women.

West Lake

For a full panorama of **West Lake** and the city, ascend the five storeys of Evening Sunlight at Thunder Peak Pagoda (Leifeng Xizhao; open daily 8am–dusk), newly rebuilt on thousand-year-old ruins on the lake's southern shore. Another vista spot is located on the summit of the hill on the north side of the lake, where the hauntingly beautiful **Baochu Pagoda** stands. It was originally built in 968, and destroyed and rebuilt several times. The present pagoda dates from 1933 and is 45m (148ft) tall.

But the beauty of the lake can best be appreciated at close range: from the deck of a sightseeing boat or from the paths and causeways along its shore. The lake edge is abundantly supplied with flowers, trees and, unusual in China, secluded places where lovers can find privacy.

The highlight of a boat trip across West Lake is the largest of three man-made islands, a 'small fairy island' known as **Three Pools Mirroring the Moon** (Santan Yinyue). The island, created in the Ming dynasty, was ingeniously provided with an island of its own, in the centre of its own lake. A zigzag bridge will get you there. Three small stone pagodas, rebuilt in the 17th century, rise from the main lake just south of the isle. On the night of the Moon Festival, candles are placed inside the pagodas. The flickering light emanating from the small round windows gives the lake 15 reflections imitating the real moon.

Solitary Hill Island (Gushan Dao), in the northern part of the lake, is reached from the city by a causeway named after a Tang dynasty poet, Baijuyi. During the 9th century he was

The 1,000-year-old Laughing Buddha of Feilaifeng

demoted from a high imperial position to the job of governor of Hangzhou because he wrote poems satirising the court (which, of course, made him extremely popular with the ordinary people). Leafy Gushan Park, in the centre of the island, was established in 1752 as a private imperial resort. The **Zhejiang Provincial Museum** on Solitary Hill (open Tues–Sun 8.30am–4.30pm) is reputed to contain 100,000 cultural relics – including the oldest grains of cultivated rice in the world, harvested around 7,000 years ago.

From Monastery to Plantation

One of the country's best-known Buddhist monasteries, Hangzhou's **Lingyin Temple** ('Spirits' Retreat', open daily 7am–5pm), west of West Lake, attracts crowds of Chinese tourists and believers. The monks – for this is a working monastery – are kept busy supplying joss (incense) sticks to devout or merely fun-loving visitors. The main hall contains a statue of the Buddha seated on a lotus leaf: carved out of camphorwood, it is 19.5m (64ft) high and thought to be the largest such sculpture in China.

Nearby, the **Peak That Flew from Afar** (Feilaifeng) shelters 380 Buddhist stone carvings created during the Yuan dynasty and four sacred caves. The most famous sculpture is of the Laughing Buddha with a bulging belly, an animated figure fashioned about 1,000 years ago.

Further southwest into the lush West Lake hills is the village of **Dragon Well** (Longjing), where Hangzhou's celebrated Longjing tea is cultivated. Villagers welcome visitors who arrive by local bus or bicycle, sharing cups of tea and selling the precious leaves.

On the way, it's worth a stop at the **China Tea Museum** (Zhongguo Chaye Bowuguan; open daily 8am–5pm), with its displays of ceremonial tea implements and its own model teahouses.

Hangzhou is also renowned for its silks. The **Hangzhou Silk Printing and Dyeing Complex** (Hang Si Lian) is the largest in China. Daily tours follow the production process from the sorting of cocoons, which arrive by barge in 20-kg (44-lb) sacks, to silk-screen printing. The **China Silk Museum** (open daily 8am–5pm) lays out the history of silk and sells bolts of the fabric.

The lakeside promenade provides plenty of shopping and small restaurants, as do Nanshan Lu and the upscale pedestrian mall Yihu Tiandi (West Lake Heaven on Earth). But the essence of Hangzhou is its scenery. The lake and hills afford some of the most scenic walking and cycling of any city in China.

HARBIN

Only a polar bear, you would think, could survive winter in Harbin, the capital of China's northeasternmost province, Heilongjiang. The average temperature stays below freezing five months of the year, and the mercury has been known to drop to -38°C (-36°F). It's no surprise that ice-sailing is popular here, or that Yabuli International Ski Resort, with China's best slopes, is nearby.

New Year ice lanterns, a speciality of Harbin

In a country of ancient cities, Harbin is an anomaly. Until the 20th century it never amounted to more than a fishing village. Then the Manchu dynasty agreed to let Tzarist Russia build a branch of the Trans-Siberian Railway through Harbin. Russians and other foreigners peopled the fast-growing transportation hub, which soon boasted hotels and banks, bars and gambling houses. With the Bolshevik revolution of 1917, perhaps half a million Russian émigrés fled through Siberia to Harbin, consolidating the Russian appearance of the city with more pastel-coloured stucco houses and churches with onion domes. From 1932 to 1945, Harbin was under Japanese occupation, followed by one year under the Soviet army. In 1946 the Chinese communists took control of the city.

Under the People's Republic, Harbin has become an important industrial centre as well as the heart of a rich grain-producing area. With its eclectic mix of Russian domes, traditional Chinese architecture and industrial concrete eyesores, Harbin is aesthetically confusing and often startling, juxtaposing the drab and mundane with the elegant and exotic.

The mighty **Songhua River**, running through the city from west to east, inevitably attracts tourists. In summer months there are sightseeing launches and, for the brave, swimming. On the south bank, **Stalin Park** (Sidalin Gongyuan) is a wide,

Lanterns of Ice

At the Chinese lunar New Year, or Spring Festival (in late January or early February), Harbin puts on its keynote event: a spectacular show that rivals the famous Snow Festival of its sister city in Japan, Sapporo. While the rest of China is celebrating the New Year with paper lanterns, Harbin is showing off with lanterns carved out of ice in its Ice Lantern Festival, held downtown in Zhaolin Park. Delicate sculptures, human figures and whole buildings meticulously carved out of ice are brilliantly illuminated. The ambience is so festive, you might even forget the sub-zero temperatures.

inviting promenade, with its Flood Control Monument the chief focal point for visitors, a curious architectural mix of classical and social realist styles. Visible from the shore is **Sun Island** (Taiyang Dao; ferries leave daily 8.20am–4.30pm), in the middle of the river, with health resorts, beach installations and gardens. Also on the island is **Siberian Tiger Park** (Dongbei Hu Linyuan; daily bus tours, 8am–6pm), where en-

Siberian Tiger Park, where these endangered cats breed

dangered Manchurian tigers, dodging the tourist buses, learn to hunt live prey before their release into the wild.

Daoli Old Town

The main walking district, the cobblestoned **Daoli Old Town** (Daoliqu), bordered by Stalin Park, retains much of Harbin's Russian heritage in its onion-domed architecture. Other attractions include the inactive but spectacular **Santa Sophia Church** (open daily 8.30am–5pm) and two active temples. Sixth-century stone tablets grace **Wenmiao**, Harbin's temple to Confucius, a charming sanctuary that contain's Harbin's only jade bridges, while Jilesi, the **Temple of Bliss**, the largest in the province, hosts an active community of monks and nuns and opens onto a large, lively street market. Both temples are open daily 8am–4pm.

One of Harbin's most delightful spots is the **Children's Park** (Ertong Gongyuan), where there is a miniature railway operated by children – the only one of its kind in China. Little trains run daily 8.30am–6.30pm carrying passengers of all ages in 20 minutes from 'Harbin Station' to 'Beijing Station', a distance of 2km (just over 1 mile).

A darker attraction altogether is the **Exhibition Hall for the Ruins of the Japanese Troops Invading China** (open daily 8–11.30am and 1–4.30pm), the site of a secret biological warfare research station set up by the occupying Japanese forces in 1939 to test on the local population. Its existence was hidden until the 1980s.

> The Japanese blew up their biological warfare centre before fleeing in 1945, so today's exhibits are limited to illustrations of the horrors this site witnessed. The strong feelings that they evoke are aggravated by controversial documents which suggest that the US spared the Japanese scientists in exchange for their research results.

HOHHOT

The capital of the Inner Mongolia Autonomous Region, Hohhot is a sprawling, booming city with a metropolitan population of more than one million. The centre of town looks to the future with new official buildings, housing blocks and wide avenues, but the traffic evokes nostalgia with its parade of donkey carts, ox carts, pony carts and farm tractors, plus the usual proliferation of bicycles.

It might come as a surprise that Mongolians are only a small minority here. Most of the residents of Hohhot are Han (ethnic Chinese), and Inner Mongolia's close connection with China dates back several centuries. For tourists in search of the exotic, though, Hohhot and the vicinity offer many opportunities to make contact with Mongolian traditions. You can drink butter tea with millet and even sleep in a *yurt*, a felt-covered circular tent.

A quite unexpected feature of Hohhot is its modern **racecourse** (saimachang), a throwback to the great equestrian tradition of the nomadic Mongols. Under the sky-blue domes of the reviewing stand, visitors are often treated to a Mongolian 'rodeo' of racing and trick riding and perhaps a procession of shaggy Bactrian camels. Another lively spot is **Xinhua Square**, where half the town seems to exercise and play before work, returning each evening to sample the kebabs and other fare from dozens of food stalls. Along nearby streets pedlars shout out their wares with equal enthusiasm, whether they're selling shirts, vegetables or sunglasses. Cobblers work hand-cranked sewing machines in the open air. A bard, banging a cymbal, chants a story, while his partner – a trained monkey – dons the masks and hats of various Chinese opera characters, mesmerising the crowd.

The **Inner Mongolia Museum** (Nei Menggu Bowuguan; open daily 9am–6pm) covers the region's history from prehistoric times to the communist revolution, with an ample display of native *yurts* and riding gear, as well as China's largest dinosaur skeleton. Among Hohhot's sacred sites, the **Xiletuzhao Temple** (Xiletuzhao Si; open daily 8am–6pm) stands out. It is an active Lamaist Buddhist shrine, with many Tibetan trappings, its main hall filled with brightly coloured dragon carpets and an overwhelming smell of incense. Attractive to photographers is the aptly named **Five Pagodas Temple** (Wutasi; open daily

The steppes of Inner Mongolia stretch as far as the eye can see

8am–6pm), a striking 18th-century structure capped with five towers. Buddhist scriptures are inscribed on the outer wall in Sanskrit, Tibetan and Mongolian, along with carvings of 1,600 figures. The astronomical chart with Mongolian inscriptions is the only one of its kind in China.

The **Great Mosque** (Qingzhen Dasi; open daily 10am–4pm), dating back to the Ming dynasty, serves the large Hui Muslim population that lives in the neighbourhood. The mosque has a minaret that culminates in a Chinese-style temple roof (topped by a crescent). The front of the prayer hall is adorned with Arabic inscriptions and ceramic abstractions. Non-Muslims are not allowed inside the various halls of worship.

Hohhot's oldest historical site, situated 17km (11 miles) southwest of town, is the **Tomb of Princess Zhaojun** (Zhaojunmu; open daily 10am–4pm). In 33BC, at the age of 18, this famous Chinese beauty married a tribal chief, thus bringing about what is now hailed as peace among the nationalities. You can take a stroll

Many Mongolians in Hohhot still live in traditional *yurts*

to the top of the 33-metre (98-ft) earthen pyramid built above her grave and, from here, look out over the endless, flat farmland.

Southeast of Hohhot is the 12th-century **White Pagoda** (Baita; open daily 8am–6pm), known in Chinese as Wanbuhua Yanjingta: the Pagoda of the Ten Thousand Scriptures. The restored seven-tier octagonal structure, isolated amid farmland, was constructed of brick about 900 years ago when it served as a centre of religious pilgrimages during the Liao Dynasty. Although the outside is brilliant white, the interior can be pitch black, making for a treacherous climb.

The Grasslands

The most memorable aspect of a visit to Hohhot is likely to be an excursion to the grasslands *(caoyuan)*, across the desolate Daqing Mountains, where horseback riding is a way of life among Mongolians. A good paved road eases the strain of the zigzag climb that continues up approximately 2,000m (more than 6,500ft) above sea level.

Most visitors end up at either **Xilamuren** or **Gegentala**, a three-hour drive from Hohhot. At these tourist camps, guests sleep in wool-felt *yurts* with quilts, hot water flasks and electric lights. Bathing facilities and dining halls are often in separate buildings. Daily activities can include archery, Mongolian wrestling, visits to local villages and horse- riding on the celebrated grasslands. Folk dancing and singing provide evening entertainment.

Traditional Naadam fairs are held in late summer, and at other times. Visitors might be treated to an informal rodeo in which Mongolian horsemen race their energetic ponies. Disarmingly, the cowboys are dressed like ordinary Chinese farmers. Tourists are then offered the chance to ride camels (stepladders are provided for mounting these mild-mannered animals) and ponies.

Travellers with more time can venture deeper into the wilderness grasslands, where there is a better chance of sleeping in a real *yurt*, not one specially furnished for foreign visitors. Other popular destinations west of Hohhot are the **Genghis Khan Mausoleum** (Chengji Sihan Lingyuan; open daily 7am–7pm) in the Ordoes

Highlands – it was actually built in 1954 and recently augmented with a reconstructed Yuan dynasty village – and the nearby **Resonant Sand Gorge** (Xiangshawan; open daily 9am–5pm) and **Wudang Lama Temple** (Wudang Zhao; open daily 8am–6pm).

HUANGSHAN

Although 'Yellow Mountain' is the literal translation of **Huangshan** (not one mountain but a range of dozens of peaks), yellow is not the colour that first comes to mind when describing this romantic site, which has been the subject of Chinese poetry and painting for centuries. In reality, green is the colour of the stunted pines clinging to purple cliff faces. Pink are the wildflowers, blue the sky, and white the sea of clouds that rolls in beneath the rocky pinnacles.

Huangshan, a UNESCO World Heritage Site, is the only region of eastern China's Anhui Province that appears on major tourist itineraries. Trains and planes link Shanghai with a terminus at the foot of the mountains, where coaches continue the journey. The scenic mountain resort now has hotel facilities, from extremely basic to comfortable. Chinese tourists – and poets – might spend a week or more exploring the area, but foreign visitors try to squeeze it all into a day or two.

The Huangshan vista that has most inspired painters and photographers is the sight of cottony clouds nuzzling the mountainsides. The peaks and pinnacles, jutting above the clouds in the early morning sky, look like islets in a celestial sea. If there's a single source for classic Chinese landscape painting, it's surely Huangshan.

The weather can be a critical factor in the pleasure of mountain rambles and sightseeing. On average, mid-July to the end of September is considered the most dependable time of year because of the mild temperatures and relatively restrained rainfall. Drizzle rather than heavy rain generally falls from late May to late

A painter's delight: the tree-clad mountains of Huangshan

June, when the spring flowers burst forth, but temperatures are brisk. Mist and fog often enhance rather than obscure the views.

Huangshan has many peaks that are well known by name in China, often through thousands of poems describing these as the country's most beautiful mountains. The three principal summits are **Lotus Flower Peak** (Lianhuafeng), **Bright Summit** (Guangmingding), and the **Heavenly Capital Peak** (Tiandufeng). All are over 1,800m (6,000ft) high and all can be climbed via endless stone stairs, some as steep as ladders. Of the three, Bright Summit is the most accessible; Lotus Flower Peak is slightly more difficult; Heavenly Capital Peak is frequently closed for safety reasons, not for the faint-hearted or safety-conscious.

Climbs begin on the east side of the range at Yungu Temple, where a cable car whisks some visitors to the summit while most begin an 8-km (5-mile) hike. At the twin summits, the Northern and Western Sea of Clouds, there are small inns and a large hotel, somewhere to get some rest before viewing the sunrise.

The descent on the west side is longer, with up to 14km (9 miles) of paths and stairs, although a cable car also serves this route. A third cable car operates on the north slope.

When hiking becomes too strenuous, Huangshan visitors can recuperate in a hot spring resort that lies between Purple Cloud Peak (Ziyunfeng) and Peach Blossom Peak (Taohuafeng). Here, piping hot water with a curative mineral content bubbles from the spring year-round. You can drink it, bathe in it, or both.

JINAN

Sweet water gushes from more than 100 springs in the late summer rainy season within the city limits of Jinan, the capital of Shandong (Shantung) Province. The water enhances agriculture

Thousand Buddha Mountain in fact accommodates around 100

and industry and even turns this 'City of Springs' into a tourist attraction. And thanks to nature's generosity, Jinan is the only city in China where you can safely drink the tap water. Even so, most visitors only pass through Jinan on their way to such traditional sights of Shandong as the holy mountain of Taishan *(see page 163)* and Qufu, the birthplace of Confucius *(see page 198)*.

The Jinan area seems to have been inhabited since the New Stone Age. More than 2,500 years ago, a town wall was built and Jinan has been a prosperous provincial capital since the medieval period. At the turn of the 20th century, the Manchu dynasty granted foreign concessions in Jinan, prompting an influx of Europeans. The city was a focus of bitter fighting during the Chinese Civil War. Today almost two million people live in the city.

Sightseeing starts among the weeping willows along the shores of the **Lake of Great Light** (Daminghu), in the northern part of the old city. In recent years the lake has been dredged and stone embankments built, and all around it are parks, playgrounds and pavilions (open daily 6am–7pm).

Southeast of the city is **Thousand Buddha Mountain** (Qianfoshan; open daily 6am–7pm), but instead of a thousand Buddha images you'll find about a hundred today. And, at only 280m (about 900ft) above sea level, it is more a hill than a mountain. But a hike up and down offers a close look at old temples, grottoes with Buddhist statues and refreshing forests of gingkos and cypresses. A cable-car runs to and from the temples (about halfway up) from 6am to 7pm, and the adventurous can descend on a slide called the 'Magical Function Skidway'.

Of all the springs in Jinan, the one with the most historical associations is the **Jet Spring** (Baotuquan). It was from this spring in the 17th century that the Qing dynasty emperor Kangxi took a swig and pronounced it the 'First Spring Under Heaven'. It is now surrounded by a carefully landscaped park. A short walk away is **Black Tiger Spring** (Heihuquan), its sweet water roaring from the mouths of three tigers carved in a black stone cliffside.

As the provincial capital, Jinan is the site of the **Shandong Provincial Museum** (open Mon–Fri 8.30am–noon and 2.30–6pm, Sat–Sun 9am–5pm), where more than 400,000 items illustrate local history and nature. The highlight of the collection is an exhibition of Longshan Black Pottery found near Jinan – an elegant, delicate ware fired 4,000 years ago. An interesting animal exhibit upstairs includes exotic birds, huge sea turtles and a freakish stuffed six-legged calf.

KAIFENG

The ancient walled city of Kaifeng, located in eastern Henan Province, lies near enough to the unpredictable Yellow River to have known more than its share of catastrophes – and when it wasn't being flooded it was being pillaged. The most terrible of the invasions, in the 12th century, extinguished the dreams of the Northern Song dynasty and left Kaifeng in ruins. All things considered, it's almost miraculous that several historic buildings have survived to this day. So, remarkably, has much of the city's old imperial dignity.

Kaifeng rose to fame more than 2,000 years ago during the Warring States period, when it was capital of the Kingdom of Wei (220–265BC). The city's most prosperous and glorious era was between the years AD960 and 1127, when it was the Eastern Capital of the Northern Song dynasty.

The **Iron Pagoda** (Tieta; open daily 7am–7pm), Kaifeng's best-known symbol, looks as if it's made of iron, but the exterior walls are faced with glazed bricks and tiles of an iron-like hue. Built in 1049 and restored in modern times, it is a lucky 13 tiers tall. It was originally part of a 6th-century monastery complex, but the other buildings were washed away in one of the great floods of the 19th century. Another relic of the Song dynasty, the

The abacus – sold in traditional stores like this – is still widely used

square and imposing **Pota** (Pagoda of the Po Family; open daily 8.30am–4.30pm) reveals none of the high-flying grace of the Iron Pagoda. This might be excused by the fact that the top three tiers of the building collapsed several hundred years ago.

In the northwest quarter of the city, the **Imperial Way** of the Song emperors has been reconstructed. Tile-roofed souvenir shops and restaurants line the street for three blocks, terminating at the entrance to **Dragon Pavilion Park** (Longtingyuan; open daily 6.30am–7pm in summer, 7am–6pm in winter). The park overlooks two scenic lakes and has a 500-m stone pathway that leads to the double-decker central pavilion, with upswept golden roofs, which was reconstructed in the 17th-century.

West from Dragon Pavilion Park along the lakeshore is the Stele Forest of the Imperial Academy, an outdoor arena with over 3,000 ancient carved tablets. Nearby is Kaifeng's newest tourist attraction, the **Qingming Park up the River** (Qingming Shanghe Yuan), a theme park modelled on a 12th-century scroll picturing festive and imperial Kaifeng.

At the centre of Kaifeng, the main attraction is the **Grand Xiangguo Monastery** (Daxiangguosi; open daily 8am–6.30pm in summer, 8am–5.30pm in winter) founded in the 6th century. Inside is the gilded statue of the 'Thousand-Armed and Thousand-Eyed Buddha', which (incredibly) has more than the advertised number of arms and eyes. Outside the temple is the city's liveliest and largest open-air market, complete with dancing monkeys.

A community of Jews migrated to Kaifeng in about the 10th century. They established a synagogue in 1163 and maintained a community until the great flood of 1852. Although they have been assimilated, as many as a hundred Kaifeng residents still claim Jewish heritage. Stone tablets recording the history of Jews in Kaifeng are stored in the Kaifeng Museum. The grounds of the **Purity and Truth Synagogue** (Youtai Jiaotang Yizhi), north of a Catholic church and east of a mosque, can still be located with the help of local guides. Bang on the doors and someone will usually let you in.

Harvest time near Kunming

KUNMING

Flights into Kunming, the capital of Yunnan Province, land on an unexpectedly long runway that has a dramatic history, commemorated neither by plaques nor monuments. This was once the end of the line for the Flying Tigers, the American pilots who supplied China during World War II. Kunming was also the Chinese terminus for supplies travelling down the tortuous Burma Road; milestone '0' – otherwise unmarked – can be seen on the right side of the road 21km (13 miles) from the centre of Kunming, on the edge of the Western Hills.

One of Kunming's best attractions is its benign climate. The city is situated at an altitude of 1,894m (more than 6,200ft), and up here temperatures are pleasantly mild, producing what is described as perpetual springtime. During one season or another the camellia, azalea, magnolia and begonia are in flower, and the region is renowned as China's pharmacopoeia. The thatched roofs of farmhouses are draped with drying corn and chilli peppers.

The total metropolitan population stands at over 3 million, of whom half live in the city proper. To make it all the more exotic, a high proportion of the citizens belong to minority nationalities and often appear in ethnic costumes. The city's leading university, the Institute for Nationalities, has over 20,000 minority students.

Downtown Kunming has modernised rapidly, but there are still a few touches of the old, the exotic and the scenic: a colourful bird and flower market, the blind masseurs who work outside in the public square at the Workers' Cultural Hall, the **Nancheng Ancient Mosque** (devotees arrive daily around 1.30pm, particularly on Fridays). A few older neighbourhoods remain around the city's main park, **Green Lake** (Cuihui), and the lake is pleasant, particularly on a Sunday when families visit and in winter when the 'laughing gulls' stop over on their way from Siberia.

Then there's Kunming's most interesting temple, Qiongzhusi, the **Bamboo Temple** (open daily 8am–7pm), 13km (8 miles) northwest of the city centre. It houses the surreal work of a 19th-century sculptor who created a version of the 500 *arhats* (followers of the Buddha) that is unequalled at any other Buddhist temple in China.

Also of considerable interest is the **Golden Temple** (Jin Dian), 10km (6 miles) northeast of town. The temple gets its name from the magnificent all-bronze hall, which weighs an incredible 250 tons. Such a hall is not unique in China – bronze temple halls can also be found in Taihuai (Wutaishan) in Shanxi and at the Summer Palace in Beijing – but this is the largest. A cable car connects the Golden Temple to the vast grounds of the International Horticultural Exposition Park below.

Lake Dian

Kunming's prime scenic and recreational area is at **Lake Dian**, China's sixth largest, where tour boats cruise the crystal waters. **Grand View Park** (Daguan Gongyuan; open daily 8am–6pm), on one shore, provides the flowers for which Kunming is famous, along with arched bridges and pavilions. On the opposite shore, the rich green slopes of the Western Hills (Xishan) rise abruptly. One newer attraction on Lake Dian is the **Yunnan Nationalities Village** (Yunnan Minzu Cun; open daily 8am–7pm), an ethnic theme park exhibiting 24 minority mini-villages, probably the best of its kind in China.

A strenuous climb up the sheer face of the Western Hills via tunnels and stair treads carved from stone ultimately leads to **Dragon Gate** (Longmen). During the Ming dynasty the emperor was carried all the way up from the lakeside by four bearers. There are several excellent places to stop and catch your breath on the way up, including a teahouse, a former concubines' residence and an emperor's temporary living quarters. The gate itself is wide enough for only one person to pass through at a time. Caves painstakingly cut into the mountainside contain colourful painted carvings, all the work of a single-minded Daoist monk of the 18th century and his followers.

The bizarre limestone 'trees' of the Stone Forest

The Stone Forest

From Kunming it's just 80km (50 miles) southeast to Yunnan's most popular scenic attraction, the **Stone Forest** (Shilin). This is an other-worldly fantasy of twisted limestone formations that comprise the world's largest natural stone maze. Geologists say the structures originated 200 million years ago with the interaction of limestone, sea water, rainwater and seismic upheavals. The bizarre pinnacles that resulted are of the distinctive type of limestone called karst, the same geology that one finds in Guilin.

The Stone Forest covers about 260 sq km (100 sq miles) of Yunnan Province, but most tourists confine themselves to a manageable area of concentrated rocks. Here there are paved paths, protective railings and a few painted signs, but it is indeed possible to lose one's way inside this massive labyrinth. Near the starting point, women from the neighbouring village (members of the Sani tribe of the Yi nationality) sell

Members of the Sani tribe act as guides in the Stone Forest

embroidered blouses, bags and assorted knick-knacks. The Sani also work as freelance guides. In an open area beyond a grove of giant bamboo is the formal entrance to the forest: a wall carved with the Chinese characters for 'Shilin'.

The biggest open space in the Stone Forest, a lawn surrounded by cherry trees, is the site of a Sani festival each June. For 48 continuous hours, the tribesmen devote themselves to singing and dancing, wrestling matches, bullfights (actually, water buffalo fighting each other), feasting and romancing. Many of the celebrants come from **Five Tree Village** (Wukeshu), across Shilin Lake from the hotel. This community of several thousand Sani residents shelters water buffalo, pigs, goats and dogs. The Sani themselves live in thatched-roof, mud-and-wattle houses.

Those who stay the night in the Stone Forest are usually entertained with a Sani folklore show. Among the instruments in the orchestra are flutes, zithers and a giant banjo with a hollow bottom. Women dancers wear red-, white-and-black conical hats, while the men sport floppy black turbans. Through song and mime they recount the legends that link their people to the otherworldly presence of the Stone Forest.

LANZHOU

Two legendary thoroughfares pass through Lanzhou: the broad, powerful Yellow River and the ancient trade route known as the Silk Road. Today the big, busy city has broad new boulevards as well as intriguing old streets of shops and houses. Adding local colour, members of minority nationalities – mostly Muslim Hui people and Tibetans – contribute their own customs, costumes and cuisine to the cosmopolitan mix. In some neighbourhoods the pavements are crowded with 'free market' pedlars and artisans.

Lanzhou is the capital of Gansu Province, which extends from the farmland of the Yellow River basin through the narrow Gansu corridor, with its steep rocky mountains, to China's far west deserts and oases. Lanzhou received its name under the Sui dynasty more than 1,000 years ago. In recent times its role as a transport centre has strengthened with the spread of the railways and air routes. Industrial development here since 1949 has transformed the city, adding vast new suburbs of oil refineries and factories. The population of the metropolitan area is now almost 3 million.

The **Gansu Provincial Museum** (Gansu Sheng Bowuguan; open Tues–Sun 9am–5pm), just across the street from the big Soviet-style Huaiyi Hotel, houses Silk Road treasures and perhaps the most famous sculpture in China, the galloping *Flying Horse of Wuwei*. With its right rear leg touching a symbolic bird, the Gansu horse is the subject of countless reproductions at home and abroad. The original bronze was found in an ancient Han dynasty tomb in Gansu Province in 1969.

For a view of the muddy, swiftly moving Yellow River and the city along its banks, go along to **White Pagoda Hill Park** (Baitashan Gongyuan; open daily 7am–sunset), once a military stronghold. The temple itself, an octagonal seven-tier structure, was rebuilt in the 15th century. **Five Springs Hill Park** (Wuquanshan Gongyuan; open daily 6am–sunset) climbs a steep mountainside on the opposite bank of the river. The springs provide water for various needs, from making tea to ensuring fertility. To break up the climb there are temples, pavilions and teahouses to visit and a big pond crossed by a crooked bridge. The temples date from the 14th century; one artefact, a 5-tonne bronze bell, was cast in 1202.

West of Lanzhou are the magnificent **Thousand Buddha Temple and Caves** (Binglingsi Shiku; open daily 8am–5pm), with hundreds of statues and some of China's best-preserved Buddhist cave art, and, at Xiahe, the **Labrang Monastery** (Labulengsi; open daily 9am–noon and 2.30–4.30pm), one of the largest and most active lamaseries outside of Tibet, with over 1,000 resident monks. Southeast of Lanzhou, requiring an overnight visit, is one of the greatest of China's Buddhist grottoes, the **Maijishan Caves** (Maijishan Shiku; open daily 8am–5pm), dating back to the 4th century.

Leshan's great seated Buddha, the largest in the world

LESHAN

From the provincial capital of Chengdu, a three-hour drive via a new motorway through populous Sichuan (Szechuan) Province ends at the town of **Leshan**, the base for visits to a monumental riverside Buddha and to one of four sacred mountains of Chinese Bud-

Fun on the Great Buddha's toes

dhism, Emeishan. A 13th-century poet wrote that the most beautiful scenery of China is found in Sichuan, and some of the best of that scenery is concentrated in Leshan. Three rivers converge and flow along the city wall, and far away in the mist rises Mt Emei.

Boats ferry visitors from Leshan to the site of the **Great Buddha** (Dafo). Whether seen from the river or, later, from the hillsides, the world's largest seated Buddha is an impressive spectacle. Carved from the cliffside by a monk starting in AD713, its height is 71m (233ft). The statue's feet are so big that a hundred people can sit on each one.

The boats tie up some distance from the Buddha and passengers climb from the shore to **Dark Green Temple** (Wuyousi), with magnificent views of the surrounding rivers and Mt Emei, the gate to Western Paradise. A pathway and suspension bridge lead back to the Great Buddha. There, the Stairs of Nine Turnings wind steeply down one side of the statue to the feet. Another honeycombed stairway carved from the cliff leads back up the other side, coming out level with the massive crown, where you have a view of the Buddha's serene and knowing countenance. More temples and caves lie on the road back to the boat landing and the buses to the sacred peak.

Mt Emei

Dubbed 'the fairest mountain among the fair mountains of the world', **Mt Emei** (Emeishan) reaches an altitude of well over

3,000m (over 10,000ft). You don't have to climb all the way to the summit of Emeishan to appreciate its charm and mystique. But the higher you go, the more chance you'll have of sighting the rich fauna of the hill forests, from gregarious golden monkeys to red pandas. This was the traditional Buddhist 'Peak of the West', the mountain shrine to countless pilgrims, emperors included.

At the foot of Mt Emei, foreshadowing the many temples ahead, are the **Crouching Tiger Temple** (Fuhusi) and the 16th-century **Loyalty to Country Temple** (Baoguosi). The latter is filled with plant life, home to many small gardens and bonsai. It also contains the Shengji Bell, reputedly the second largest in China (after Beijing's Great Bell), inscribed with Buddhist scripture. There are monasteries and famous scenic spots every few kilometres along the paths to the summit, but this is a climb (for the energetic only) that requires several days. Many tourists have time to spend only a night on the mountain in one of the basic inns, such as those at the **Shrine of Limpid Waters** (Jinshui), before being driven to the summit before dawn to see the famous sunrise.

At sunrise on Golden Peak (Jinding) pilgrims and tourists alike gather in the hope of seeing an optical phenomenon called 'Buddha's Halo'. Here you can see your shadow perfectly framed inside a bright halo formed when the morning sea of clouds below Suicide Precipice is penetrated by the rising sun.

LUOYANG

Luoyang ranks among China's lesser known ancient capitals, although during the Sui dynasty 1,400 years ago, it shared the imperial court with Chang'an (present-day Xi'an). Those were the days of imperial splendour and glory. Luoyang is sometimes known as the Capital for Nine Dynasties, reflecting a political and cultural prominence that originated nearly 4,000 years ago.

In the 10th century the imperial court moved from Luoyang to the northeast. Luoyang later became capital of the central province of Henan, but by the 20th century it was merely a shadow of its former self. After the communists took power, they decided to revive the small, sleepy city as a model industrial centre. Hundreds of new factories were built, turning out tractors, mining equipment, ball bearings and thousands of other products. The city is also associated with the peony, Empress Wu Zetian's favourite flower: the annual Peony Festival every April showcases more than 500 varieties in the Royal City Park (Wangcheng Gongyuan).

The **Luoyang Museum** (Luoyang Bowuguan; open daily 8.30am–6.30pm), housed in a Ming dynasty temple, contains the fossil of an elephant tusk half a million years old, Stone-Age pottery, Shang bronzes and glazed Tang ceramic figures. The **Ancient Tombs Museum** (Gumu Bowuguan; open daily 8.30am–6pm) displays more than 20 royal tombs from the Song Dynasty. But Luoyang's most precious relics are to be found outside of town.

A short distance east of Luoyang is **White Horse Temple** (Baimasi; open daily 8.30am–7pm), China's first Buddhist monastery, which dates from the 1st century AD. The name refers to two envoys returning from India with China's first Buddhist scriptures on the backs of white horses. The texts were the first to be translated from Sanskrit into Chinese.

The Longmen Caves

Counted among the most precious of the grotto complexes in China, the **Longmen Caves** (Longmen Shiku; open daily 8am–6pm) lie about 14km (9 miles) south of Luoyang. The name Longmen, which means 'Dragon's Gate', might derive from the lie of the land here: cliffs stand like gate towers on either side of the River Yi. The best time to visit the caves is in the early morning, when the rising sun lights up the contours of the statues, giving them an eerie, lifelike quality.

The hard rock here is conducive to delicate carving, which was carried out on a monumental scale for about 400 years from AD494. More than 1,300 grottoes were constructed, as well as 2,100 niches and nearly 100,000 statues. These range from a height of about 17m (56ft) to a fingernail-sized 2cm (less than

The Longmen Caves contain more than 100,000 statues and images

an inch). In addition, there are 40 pagodas and more than 3,600 inscribed steles or tablets, of keen interest to historians and calligraphers. Some priceless sculpture was in the past looted by Europeans and Americans. Guides often point out one wall from which two classic reliefs were chiselled in 1935 'by a Chinese curio dealer bribed by an American'. The works ended up in museums in New York and Kansas City.

Some of the earliest constructions were the three Binyang Grottoes, dedicated to an emperor and empress of the Northern Wei dynasty (AD386–534), after the capital was transferred to Luoyang. The principal sculpture, five times life-size, displays features typical of that dynasty's Buddhist art: a thin face, large eyes, straight nose and quiet smile. An inscription reports that these works required the labour of 802,366 craftsmen.

The subtleties of Tang-dynasty art can be seen in the 7th-century **Ancestor Worshipping Temple** (Fengxian Si), the largest cave at Longmen, with a beautiful, exposed, 17-m (56-ft) tall Buddha statue seated on top of a 1,000-petalled lotus and accompanied by lesser, but equally brilliant, statues of disciples and guardians. The main Buddha's ears are 2m (6ft 6in) long. Completed during the reign of the Tang emperor Gaozong, the statue's face is said to be that of empress Wu Zetian, a famous patron of Buddhism at whose behest the grotto was carved. The fierce, heavenly guardian trampling a devil underfoot is thought to bring good luck to those who put their arms around the ankle, but an iron fence keeps most onlookers at bay; many other statues in other caves are similarly fenced off in a bid to preserve them. Another cave of great interest is the **Cave of Ten Thousand Buddhas** (Wanfodong), with 15,000 little Buddhas and Bodhisattvas carved into myriad niches.

Probably the oldest and one of the most beautiful of the grottoes is Guyang, begun in 495 and completed under the Northern Qi in 575. The Buddha depicted here is guarded by two magnificent lions at his feet, and the Buddha's head is a Qing dynasty replacement. A great curiosity of the complex is the Grotto of Prescriptions (Yaofangdong), begun in 575. The 120 inscriptions carved on a stone tablet here amount to a compendium of ancient Chinese illnesses and treatments.

NANJING (NANKING)

Nanjing, a booming city of around 5 million, is about 300km (185 miles) west of Shanghai in Jiangsu Province. Here the great Yangzi River narrows to slightly more than 1km (1,000yds), so even before there was a bridge the city had great strategic significance. Visitors are usually advised to avoid Nanjing in July and August, when the heat can become debilitating; temperatures of 40°C (104°F) are not uncommon.

This ancient capital of China has suffered so many catastrophes that few historic monuments have survived – and these are widely dispersed. Perhaps this is why so much emphasis is placed on modern triumphs, such as the heroic bridge across the Yangzi River that has become Nanjing's emblem. But past and present are often juxtaposed in Nanjing, like the blue pedicabs sharing the streets with big new buses, or the fresh pink and white plum blossoms on the hillsides around the Mingxiaoling tomb.

Nanjing means 'Southern Capital', a name conferred rather late in the city's history. During its early grandeur under the State of Chu, the town was called Jinling, a name still used in literary and other allusions. Then in the 3rd century, in the era of the Three Kingdoms, it was named Jianye. Under that or similar titles it served as the capital of six southern dynasties. The Ming emperors made it the national capital, but this was moved north to Beijing in the 15th century.

In the 20th century a series of dramas overtook Nanjing and gave it new prominence. It was here that Dr Sun Yat-sen was elected president of the republic. Chiang Kai-shek made it his capital until the advance of Japanese invasion forces induced him to head west. When the Japanese troops finally arrived here in 1937, the 'Rape of Nanking' was added to the catalogue of the war's atrocities. The **Datusha Jinianguan** monument and

Nanjing's emblem: the longest bridge over the mighty Yangzi River

museum (open daily 8am–5pm), just outside the old city wall commemorates the victims; around 100,000 died in the first four days alone. The nationalists regained the battered city after the Japanese surrender in 1945. The communist army crossed the Yangzi (which the Chinese people call Changjiang, or 'Long River') in April 1949, bringing the new order to the old capital.

Nanjing Sights

The **Yangzi River Bridge** (Nanjing Changjiang Daqiao) is an extraordinary engineering achievement. Only a few bridges span the entire river, and this is the longest at 1,577m (5,174ft). Proudly claimed to be the world's longest two-tier bridge for rail and road traffic, it has greatly improved contacts between North and South China. And it inspired national self-confidence at the time of the Sino-Soviet schism of 1960. When the Soviet Union withdrew its technical experts, the Chinese finished it themselves, in eight years. Today it remains an important symbol for Nanjing, although there is also now a brand-new bridge 11km (7 miles) downstream from the original.

Nanjing claims a little-known distinction – the longest **city wall** in the world. In the 14th century, the Ming rulers mobilised 200,000 workers to build fortifications extending 33.5km (nearly 21 miles). It was a formidable redoubt, with tunnels for 3,000 besieged defenders, and was never taken by enemies. The largest of 24 city gates, newly renovated as a tourist attraction, is the **Zhonghua Gate** (Zhonghuamen; open daily 8am–5.30pm), on the southern edge of Nanjing. It is a good reference point for navigating the city.

Also in southern Nanjing, you can see the ruins of the **Palace of the Heavenly King** (Tianqangfu), built when the forces of the Taiping Rebellion captured the city (*see page 36*). It was the most ambitious architectural project of the mid-19th century. The Western Garden is full of fine touches: an imaginative rock garden, a dragon wall, a children's maze, a bottle-shaped lake for an imperial stone houseboat and a fine museum chronicling the Taiping Rebellion.

The **Nanjing Museum** (Nanjing Bowuguan; open daily 9am–5pm), founded in 1933, is located inside Zhongshan Gate, the main eastern portal of the city wall. Among art and artefacts from prehistoric times to the end of the empire, the museum displays colourful ancient pottery, jade, ceramics, lacquerware, textiles, bronzes, porcelain, stone figures and a famous burial suit that is 2,000 years old. It is made from 2,600 green jade rectangles sewn together with silver wire.

Back in town, the Ming dynasty **Drum Tower** (Gulou; open daily 8am–midnight) has been restored to its eminence on a hill in the very centre of Nanjing. The drum (since replaced) told the time and warned the citizens of danger. Now there's a tearoom upstairs and a viewing deck. Nearby Gulou Park is open till 10pm and fills with families on balmy evenings.

Nanjing: buying lanterns for the New Year celebrations

One of the city's liveliest temples is **Fuzimiao** (open daily 8am–9pm), an ancient Confucian temple located in the heart of Nanjing's main shopping district and pedestrian mall; it is especially interesting to stroll through the area after working hours, when lively market stalls sell everything from parakeets to cheap clothing.

Nanjing's distinguished history as a political and cultural centre accounts for its considerable local pride. One area in which rivalry is freely revealed is the realm of cooking. Nanjing claims its salted duck is superior to the more famous Peking duck. Nanjing ducks, it is pointed out, are raised naturally on ponds, not force-fed like their less fortunate Beijing comrades.

Around Nanjing

Chinese pilgrims of all political persuasions come from many countries to honour the founder of the Chinese Republic at the **Mausoleum of Dr Sun Yat-sen** (Zhongshanling; open daily 7am–6pm), in the Purple Hills (Zijin Shan) east of Nanjing. The hillside complex roofed with blue tiles, completed in 1929, could scarcely be more grandiose. Following a long winding avenue planted with plane trees, you continue up the 392 granite steps of the ceremonial staircase to the actual memorial hall. There are statues of Dr Sun standing, sitting (by a French sculptor, Paul Landowski), and recumbent above the vault itself. On the ceiling is a mosaic version of the nationalist (Guomindang) flag, a white star on a blue background.

The grandiose Mausoleum of Sun Yat-sen, Nanjing

Dr Sun often roamed these hills during his Nanjing years. It was his own wish that he be buried here, although he could never have anticipated the imperial splendour that developed.

Nearby in the Purple Hills is **Mingxiaoling** (open daily 7am–6pm), the tomb of Emperor Hong Wu, founder of the Ming dynasty. What with wars and revolutions, there is not much left of the 14th-century complex. But don't miss the **Sacred Way,** lined with large stone statues of elephants, camels, horses, lions and mythical animals, which turns north into an approach road guarded by statues of generals and mandarins. In the hall above the burial site are pictures of the emperor. Guides report he was even uglier in real life; two court artists are said to have lost their heads for an excess of realism in their portraits.

Despite its long history, Nanjing is most remembered today for its role in 20th-century events. The Yangzi Bridge, the Sun Yat-sen Memorial and the 'Rape of Nanjing' epitomise for many the essence of

The first Ming emperor Hong Wu (1327–98) was taking no chances: he had his tomb, Ming-xiaoling, built years before his death. When he died, he was buried here along with his empress and 46 concubines sacrificed for the occasion.

Nanjing. So, too, perhaps does **Meiling Palace** (Meilinggong; open daily 8.30am–5pm), the holiday home of Chiang Kai-shek and his wife Song Meiling, now open as a period museum for those nostalgic for the pre-Revolutionary days between the Last Emperor of the Manchus and the First Chairman of the Communist Party.

QINGDAO (TSINGTAO)

Imagine Copacabana beach set down on the shore of the Yellow Sea, mix in some century-old German villas and castles, and paint in pinewoods, parks and tree-lined hills for background. This world-class resort setting is one of the surprises of Qingdao, an important seaport situated on the Shandong Peninsula. Six beaches make this delightful city one of China's favourite summer retreats, as well as the site of sailing events in the 2008 Summer Olympics. The sea is refreshing and so, usually, is the air, cooled in summer by the northerly ocean currents. Whether or not you decide to join the Chinese masses and take the plunge, you'll appreciate the chance to see them at ease – sunbathing, strolling, having their pictures taken and eating ice cream or dumplings.

As you might deduce from the European architecture of the railway station and many other buildings here, Qingdao has an unusual history. Until the end of the 19th century, there was little here apart from fishermen's houses and a minor Chinese naval base. When Germany entered the imperialist age under Kaiser Wilhelm II, Qingdao was selected as a likely port for development. The murder of two German missionaries by Boxers in 1897 gave Wilhelm the excuse for a show of retaliation. German military superiority quickly forced the Manchu government into an agreement to lease the surrounding Bay of Jiaozhou to Germany.

Qingdao's railway station, built in the German style

Very soon a modern, German-style city was constructed at Qingdao, with villas, a deep-water port, a cathedral and a main street called Kaiser Wilhelmstrasse. Business was not everything: the Germans used Qingdao as a missionary base, too. It remains one of China's more Christian cities. The twin-spired 1934 **Catholic cathedral** (Tianzhu Jiaotang; open daily 8am–5pm, services Sun 7am and 6pm) and the 1908 **Protestant church** (Jidu Jiaotang; open daily 8–11.30am and 1.30–4.30pm, service Sun 9am) tend to be crowded with local people on Sundays and have become tourist attractions.

German Qingdao suffered a curious fate during World War I. Japan, which joined the Allied forces, invaded the city, imprisoned the survivors of the German garrison and occupied Qingdao for the duration of the war. China wasn't able to regain sovereignty until 1922. After the communists came to power in 1949, industrial development went forward. Despite having an urban population of nearly 2 million and a well developed commercial sector in the east, Qingdao keeps its quiet allure.

As permanent as any of the German contributions to Qingdao is its brewing prowess. The local beer has become China's national brew, exported worldwide in big green bottles or modern cans under the old spelling of the town's name, Tsingtao. Brewery tours can be arranged, and the Qingdao International Beer Festival in mid-August has become China's first attempt at an *Oktoberfest*.

German Town

Qingdao is a remarkably walkable city. Some of the German architecture is concentrated in the Badaguan District on Taiping Bay, near Beach No. 1. This is a lovely neighbourhood of Western-style mansions, landscaped lawns and tree-lined lanes, capped by what can only be described as a German castle by the sea – the governor's lodge during colonial days (Huashi Lou; open daily 8am–6pm).

Not far from the old villas and castle is **Qianhai Pier**, once the main berth for German ships. Now the pier has been lengthened to an impressive 440m (nearly a quarter of a mile), and an octagonal pavilion lies at the far end. Visitors and vendors alike crowd the promenade. Roving portrait photographers hustle tourists, pitching the lighthouse as a background.

Above the beaches, with fine views of the city and the sea, are a number of parks atop steep green hills. In Xinhao Park there stands the opulent residence built for the German governor in 1903. Formerly a hotel, the **Qingdao Welcome Guest House** (Qingdao Ying Binguan; open daily 8.30am–4.30pm) now serves as a period museum. The grand piano in its plush lobby, dated

1876, is German, but the former suites off the lobby area are decidedly Chinese. Occupied for a month in 1957 by Chairman Mao and his wife, they remain just as Mao left them decades ago, including his desk which has a secret compartment.

In addition to Qingdao's stunning beaches, which attract some 100,000 sunbathers every summer, the area is renowned for the mountain resort of **Laoshan**, 40km (nearly 25 miles) to the east. Bordering the sea, Laoshan is rich in legends, springs, waterfalls and steep trails. Laoshan mineral water, of vaunted medicinal value, originates here and is sold throughout China. Once the site of 72 temples, Laoshan still has an interesting temple by the sea, **Xiaqinggong**, a Daoist retreat that dates back to 14BC.

> **Qingdao is best known in the West for its most famous export, Tsingtao beer, brewed here since 1903. (The brewery, in Dengzhoulu, is open daily for groups only.) The brewers maintain that the beer's high quality is due not only to German brewing expertise but also to the spring water used, from Laoshan Mountain.**

SHANGHAI

You couldn't confuse Shanghai with anywhere else in China. It is bigger, more prosperous and more dynamic than any other city; its skyline boasts European-style towers; its shop windows and food stalls seize your attention. Through the late 1990s, Shanghai was the world's boomtown, rebuilding itself and growing far faster than any other major city. It required so many construction cranes that there was a regional shortage in the rest of Asia. It has become a city of more than 3,100 high-rise buildings, and the pace of construction is slowing only slightly.

Before war and revolution changed its face, Shanghai was dominated by foreign fortune-hunters, social climbers and a glittering array of sinners. Its very name became a verb in

English: 'to shanghai' means to abduct by trickery or force. Nowadays it is regaining much of its old glamour, albeit without the disreputable edge.

With 17 million people (depending on how you count), Shanghai is one of the most extensive cities in the world. The dynamic city metropolitan area covers about 6,000 sq km (more than 2,300 sq miles), which is five times the size of the city of Los Angeles. Administered as a separate region, like Beijing, the Shanghai metropolis includes rich farmland as well as big-city housing complexes and heavy industry. It is not only extensive but expensive: a recent cost-of-living survey ranked Shanghai as the sixth most expensive city in the world, ahead of London, Geneva and New York.

Nanjing Road, Shanghai's most famous shopping street

The population, China's most worldly, fashionable and open people, are very individualistic, speaking a dialect that nobody else can understand, eating a different cuisine and generally considering themselves to be light years ahead of their nearest competitor, Beijing (and catching up fast with Hong Kong). Shanghai's higher living standard, pulsating night-life and cosmopolitan air can make the capital seem rather dowdy in comparison.

Shanghai's present position as a great industrial and commercial centre is part of an earlier 19th and 20th-century colonial tradition. The city has retained a special appeal to visitors as a sophisticated, busi-

Modern Shanghai has more than 3,000 high-rise buildings

nesslike metropolis – made all the more colourful because of its nostalgic associations.

Shanghai in History

China's prime port began unpromisingly 1,000 years ago as a fishing village on mud flats near the Yangzi River's outlet to the East China Sea. Shanghai didn't officially become a town until the 13th century, but even then it was largely ignored by the rest of China – but not by Japanese pirates, who were attracted by the overseas trade that passed through the town. After numerous attacks, in the 16th century Shanghai built a protective wall which surrounded the old city until 1912.

In the 17th and 18th centuries, domestic commerce increased the importance of Shanghai as a port and marketplace. But the authorities firmly resisted foreign connections until British gunboats won an invitation. After the 1842 Opium War, Shanghai became one of five Chinese ports open to foreign residence and trade. Over the next few years the influx of Europeans, Americans and refugees from the battles of the Taiping Rebellion turned Shanghai into a glamorous, if naughty, trading port. Foreign concession areas took up most of what is now central Shanghai, except for the old walled Chinese part of the city. Soon Shanghai became the place to be – a city with the best culture, the most opulent dance halls, the largest volume of business, the tallest buildings. But little of the prosperity filtered down to the ordinary citizen, who was kept apart.

Bitterness at the injustices and corruption of Shanghai society fired the city's revolutionary movement: the Chinese Communist Party was founded here in 1921.

Between 1937 and 1945, Shanghai was occupied by Japanese troops; most of the foreign colony was interned. After the war the Guomindang nationalists took power, but communist troops seized Shanghai in 1949. The new regime wiped out organised crime and vice, expropriated factories and built new ones, setting the city on a new industrial course. In 1965 the Cultural Revolution was sparked off in Shanghai, as the political base of Jiangqing, the former Shanghai actress who was Mao's wife. Despite the Red Guards' enthusiasm for demolishing anything that was not defined as Socialist Realism, many buildings from colonial times have survived in the city. After the death of Mao and the arrest of the Gang of Four, Shanghai culture and art experienced a renaissance, and the new economic policies of the reform era benefited Shanghai more than any other city.

The Port and Bund

As an essentially 19th-century phenomenon, Shanghai matured too late to contribute to classical Chinese art or culture. Although historic monuments are relatively rare here, it doesn't mean the city lacks for sights.

In Shanghai the interest shifts to relics of uninhibited pre-war capitalism and scenes of the city's contemporary energy and flair.

Shanghai's Grand Theatre

The port of Shanghai sums up the strange and often uncomfortable meeting of East and West, of old and new. The muddy Huangpu River slices through the centre of the city, after passing through the seemingly interminable

The Bund retains a certain European elegance

industrial suburbs complete with their fuming smokestacks. Foghorns converse into the night, long after the sound of car horns and bike bells has ceased. The river traffic is a motley flotilla of modern container ships and ocean-going junks – their sails the colour of grime – of packed ferries and convoys of barges, warships, rusty coasters and bobbing sampans. Visitors can take a comfortable and endlessly fascinating riverboat tour of the Huangpu from downtown Shanghai to the mouth of the Yangzi River.

Returning to the city, in the almost inevitable haze, you see the astonishingly un-Chinese skyline of Shanghai, a mythical European metropolis transplanted to the Orient. The Waitan, the riverfront promenade on the left bank of the Huangpu, used to be called the **Bund** (and still is by many), from an Anglo-Indian word for an embankment on a muddy shore. It's easy to imagine the elegance of the Bund in its heyday, when the gardens were barred to dogs and Chinese, in that order. This is the place for relaxed people-watching, from early morning when the shadow-boxers work out, until the evening strolls of well-dressed courting couples. The promenade has been widened, and the stretch is now home to smart restaurants and shopping centres.

Facing the river along Zhongshan Road are some grandiose old buildings that are undergoing restoration and reoccupation. These include the Peace Hotel; the Seamen's Club, formerly the British consulate; and the massive 1923 headquarters of the old Hong Kong and Shanghai Bank, recently renovated and transformed into a Chinese bank, eliminating the separate entrances for Chinese and Europeans. And east across the river is new East Shanghai, known as Pudong, where construction is booming and where you can enjoy a view from the top of one of Asia's tallest structures.

Around Nanjing Road

One of the pleasures of Shanghai is to stroll Nanjing Road, long the most famous shopping avenue in China, to see what's new and what's old. Pop into the **Peace Hotel** (Heping Fandian) on the Bund and peruse the art-deco lobby. This is where Noel Coward holed up to write *Private Lives* and where Steven Spielberg filmed scenes for *Empire of the Sun*. The Peace Hotel's jazz band, performing here since the 1930s, still swings every evening in the north wing.

North from the Bund is the **Ohel Moshe Synagogue** (Moxihuitang), built in 1927 to serve Shanghai's Jewish population, which once numbered 20,000. No longer a functioning synagogue, it now houses a small museum (open daily 9am–4.30pm).

On the south side of Nanjing Road is **People's Park** (Renmin Gongyuan), once home to the Shanghai Race Track (1863) and now adjacent to the elegant and newly renovated **Shanghai Art Museum** (Shanghai Meishu Guan; open daily 9am–5pm). **People's Square** (Renmin Guangchang) houses the lavish Grand Theatre, the illuminating Shanghai Urban Planning Exposition

The former Hong Kong and Shanghai Bank on the Bund

Admiring calligraphy in the Shanghai Museum

Centre and the incomparable **Shanghai Museum** (Shanghai Bowuguan; open Sun–Fri 9am–5pm, Sat 9am–8pm), which is the best in China, especially in terms of its state-of-the-art displays and presentation. There are four floors of exhibits with stalls on each floor selling gifts and museum reproductions. Bronzes and stone sculptures are on the ground floor, ceramics are on the first, paintings and calligraphy are on the second floor, and coins, jade and furniture are on the third. Not all of the museum's 120,000 artefacts can be displayed here at one time, but many visitors savour these displays and insist upon a return visit. For a break during museum browsing, there's a lovely tearoom on the first floor.

The Old City

Just southwest of the Bund is a district known today as the Old City (Nanshi), within the circle formed by Renminlu and Zhonghualu. Shanghai's city walls ran parallel to this ring road until they were knocked down in 1912. Then the moats were filled in and today's streets laid down. Before 1949 the Old City remained under Chinese law and administration, while the rest of Shanghai was carved up by foreign powers, and most of the residents in these old back alleys were Chinese. Eventually it became notorious as a gangster-and-opium slum. Today the vices are gone but the crowded neighbourhoods, and some of the small houses and tiny lanes still exist.

In the heart of the Old City, on Fuyoulu, the **Yuyuan Garden** (open daily 8.30am–5pm) was commissioned by a Ming dynasty mandarin. As the main classical Chinese garden in

Shanghai, it is an absolute gem of landscaping and architecture – the perfect place for local people to seek tranquillity, so conveniently offered in the heart of old Shanghai. If you visit only one classic garden in China, this is the best single choice.

Just inside the main gate is a rockery, an artificial hill of inherently interesting stones, held together with glutinous rice powder and lime. From the pavilion on top of this hill, the Ming official could watch all the excitements of river life, though tall buildings now intervene. In front of the **Hall of Ten Thousand Flowers** grows a 400-year-old gingko tree. Another carefully created rockery is reflected in a pond teeming with giant goldfish. All the corridors and pavilions, bridges and walls, sculptures and trees are so artfully arranged that the garden seems many times larger than its actual, compact size.

The Yuyuan Garden, an oasis of peace in the city's chaos

Outside the garden walls, a large rectangular pond is bisected by the Nine Turnings Bridge, so shaped to deflect evil spirits. The bridge is the only link to the 400-year-old **Huxinting Teahouse** (257 Yuyuanlu; open daily 8.30am–10pm), which lies in the centre of an illuminated pond. With its upswept roofs, this is an irresistible stop for soem refreshing tea and snacks. There's no prettier teahouse in all of China.

The teahouse pond marks one corner of the Old Chinese City (Nanshi), once deemed a danger zone for European

Shanghai Old Street

visitors. You might still get lost in this maze of backstreets, reminiscent of a North African *souk*, but much of it has been renovated, tastefully, into the **Yuyuan Shopping Centre**. However there are still shops from the old bazaar days selling chopsticks, medicines, bamboo fans, silk and incense.

Also redeveloped nicely is the **Temple to the Town Gods** (Chenghuangmiao; open daily 8.30am–dusk), which dates back to the 15th century and now hosts street fairs within sight of the teahouse and Yuyuan Garden, as it did in previous centuries. On the southern edge of the Old City is the restored **Shanghai Old Street** (Fangbang Zhonglu), a quaint lane packed with teahouses and antiques shops.

The French Quarter

West of the riverside and old Chinese section is a landmark of modern history – the low brick building at **76 Xingyelu** (open daily 9am–5pm), where the Chinese Communist Party was founded in July 1921. This building was in the French concession, and when the French police learnt of the clandestine meeting, they raided the two-storey corner house. But they arrived too late to find the 12 conspirators, including Mao Zedong. The house is today a museum with documents and displays. Located adjacent is **Xin Tian Di** (New Heaven and Earth), Shanghai's most upscale pedestrian mall. Xin Tian Di is both a gourmet's delight and a functioning museum of the city's 1930s villa architecture.

Indeed, much of the finest European architecture in Shanghai can be seen in the French Quarter, where art deco and Tudor villas, neo-Gothic offices and large elegant mansions line many of the small streets. The modern Garden Hotel (58 Maominglu) preserves the original lobby area of the Cercle Sportif Français from the 1920s. The **Shanghai Museum of Arts and Crafts** (open daily 9am–4pm) is housed in a wonderful old French mansion (79 Fenyanglu) and allows visitors to view artisans at work on embroidery, paper cutting and other crafts.

Nearby, at 1555 Huaihaizhonglu, the **New Shanghai Library** (Shanghai Tushuguan; open daily 9am–5pm), one of the world's largest with over 13 million volumes, has a collection of rare books dating back 1,400 years and a reading room for foreign-language books.

Other old buildings open to view include Song Ching Ling's Former Residence (Songqingling Guju), where the wife of Sun Yat-sen lived until 1963, and Sun Yat-sen's Former Residence (Sunzhongshan Guju), where the founder of the Chinese Republic lived until 1924. The Xujiahui Cathedral, a Gothic church erected in 1848, now holds Masses in Chinese.

'New' Shanghai: Pudong

Immediately across the river from the Bund and old Shanghai is the future – the Pudong New Development Zone (Pudong Xinqu). The area was home to 1 million farmers before the government designated it the future technology and financial capital of all China. Skyscrapers designed by noted architects from around the world have replaced the farms. Shanghai's stock exchange – the first in post-Revolution China – relocated in Pudong, and the city's main international airport is there, too.

The majority of Shanghai's skyscrapers are located in Pudong, in the new East Shanghai. With its 88 storeys, one of China's tallest buildings is here: the 427-m (1,400-ft) **Jinmao Plaza**. The 468-m (1,535-ft) high **Pearl of the Orient TV Tower** (Shanghai Mingzhu; open daily 9am–9pm) might be considered a soulless and uninspiring structure, but the high-altitude observation deck is one of Shanghai's biggest tourist draws. You can also find the **Municipal History Museum**, focusing on colonial-era Shanghai, in the basement.

On Zhangyang Lu stands Asia's largest shop, the **Yaohan Department Store** (Nextage), which is 10 storeys high and sells everything from clothing to cars. Pudong even has its own version of the Bund's shore-walk in the **Riverside Promenade**. By 2010, when Shanghai hosts a World Expo, Pudong is set to be the site of the world's tallest building and a raft of new museums.

Architects from around the world contributed to Pudong's skyline

Outlying Sights

The **Jade Buddha Temple** (Yufosi; open daily 8.30am–5pm), in northwest Shanghai, is not old, but it is Shanghai's leading Buddhist site and quite active, with about 70 resident monks. Its Song dynasty-style grounds house two priceless white jade Buddha statues, one reclining, the other in the seated position of enlightenment. They were brought from Burma in 1882 and installed in the temple when it was completed in 1918. Most statues in Buddhist temples are moulded from clay with a thin overlay of gold, so these giant jade works attract curiosity seekers as well as worshippers. Around the back of the altar is a flamboyant three-dimensional mural. As an extra attraction for tourists, there's an antiques shop in the compound with some unusual items at interesting prices, and a public restaurant run by the monks.

Shanghai's only ancient pagoda, part of the lively **Longhua Temple** (Longhuagusi; open daily 6.45am–5pm) complex in the southwest suburbs, was rebuilt more than 1,000 years ago. The bell in the Bell Tower can be struck three times for a fee and sounds in the New Year at a large celebration.

Entertainment and Cuisine

Two popular venues for the performing arts in the city are the **Shanghai Centre Theatre** (which also includes the Shanghai Acrobatic Theatre) and the massive new **Grand Theatre** (Dajuyuan), Shanghai's answer to the Sydney Opera House, which showcases everything from Irish dancing to Russian ballet. The Yifu Theatre near People's Square presents both traditional Beijing opera and Shanghai's own Hu style opera on Sunday afternoons.

And then there's Shanghai cuisine. While popular local dishes are based on beancurd, together with mushrooms and bamboo shoots, the best-known Shanghai recipes capitalise on the city's proximity to the sea. Steamed freshwater crabs, in season from October through to December, and river eel are the highlights for many gourmets.

SHAOLIN

The fighting monks in a thousand kung fu films can trace their origin to the Shaolin Monastery in Henan Province. In fact, the Chinese martial arts and such offshoots as the gentler exercise forms known as *taijiquan* (tai chi) have their symbolic, if not literal, birthplace at this monastery. The branch of Buddhism known as Chan (Zen in Japan and the West) also looks to Shaolin as its source.

 With so many traditional arts centred at one historic site, it's no wonder the **Shaolin Monastery** (open daily 6am–6.30pm in summer, 8am–5.30pm in winter) has become one of China's more popular tourist attractions. Shaolin now provides movie sets for film crews as well as schools for domestic and foreign classes in self-defence. As an excursion, it is close to Zhengzhou (80km/50 miles to the east) and Luoyang (70km/43 miles west). It sits at the western edge of Songshan, the central peak of China's five sacred Daoist mountains.

The monastery is the home of most Asian martial arts. Be it kung fu or karate, taekwondo or judo, they all originated in ancient China as fighting techniques of one individual against another. It all started with the Indian monk Bodhidharma, who

Tai Chi

Tai Chi combines meditation with physical exercise, but leaves out the 'combat' element common to most other martial arts. It is practised by an individual using 'postures' that mimic techniques of attack and defence, such as 'ward-off' and 'elbow strike'. The movements are thought to have been formulated by a monk named Zhang San Feng in the 14th century, but the basic principles of Tai Chi are reflected in the instructions of the Daoist sage Lao Tse: 'Yield and Overcome; Bend and be straight.' A probable precursor to the art was a system of exercises introduced during the Three Kingdoms period and imitating certain animal movements to help exercise every joint in the body.

Shaolin boxers need to be quick, powerful and flexible

came to Songshan in AD527 and founded the monastery. He realised that many Buddhist monks were unable to maintain the total concentration necessary for their demanding meditation exercises. To aid them, he devised a physical training routine, based on his observation of animals' movements, that was designed to concentrate the mind and the body together. From this evolved the inimitable Shaolin boxing that is still practised here today, which in turn gave rise to all the other Oriental self-defence disciplines.

You don't have to be a kung fu practitioner to enjoy Shaolin. Although it is crowded and commercialised, the monastery is still one of China's most interesting historical and religious monuments. In 625 it was expanded by a Tang dynasty emperor in gratitude for wartime services rendered by the Shaolin monks, who used their fighting skills to send off some usurpers. In the 16th century the monks were called upon again to rid China's coast of Japanese pirates.

In 1928, when warlords carved up sections of the faltering Chinese Republic, one general laid siege to the monastery and set it ablaze. It was ransacked again by the Red Guards during the Cul-

It is said the Bodhidharma, the founder of the Shaolin monastery, sat facing the back wall of a cave and meditated for nine years, until his silhouette was finally imprinted on the rock.

tural Revolution, and remained closed for years. Now restored, it houses about 70 monks.

The Shaolin Monastery has a number of interesting relics and remains. Of the many halls, pavilions and temples linked by broad courtyards, the most important is the **Thousand Buddha Hall** (Qianfo Dian), dating back to 1588, with its fresco of monks engaging in battle. In the rear of the hall is a sacred stone floor, heavily dented, where generations of leaping monks are said to have left the imprint of their training. Nearby is the Shadow Stone, a slab with the outlines of a figure in meditation, said to be from the cave where The Bodhidharma meditated so steadfastly for nine years that he left his shadow on the wall. A 10-minute hike up the northern hill behind the Shaolin complex leads to the cave, now a shrine for the faithful.

The outer courtyards of Shaolin contain other unusual treasures. The **Forest of Stupas** (Shaolin Talin) is of historic note. Stupas (or dagobas) are small sealed pagodas that hold holy relics and the remains of important monks. The forest of 227 stupas at Shaolin covers over 1,000 years of Buddhist funerals, beginning with that of a Tang dynasty abbot who was buried here in 746. Adjacent to the Forest of Stupas is the most popular display at Shaolin, a courtyard of open-air pavilions containing scores of wooden statues – monks in all the classic poses of a feverish kung fu battle.

Shaolin offers one more treat for the more adventurous, for the monastery is located at the foot of the western range of the **Songshan Mountains**, part of the mountain cluster that was traditionally regarded as the Central Mountain at the centre of the Chinese Empire. A gondola now whisks visitors to the top, where hiking trails are abundant and views of the Shaolin complex and the vast desert plains of Henan are impressive. On the far side of the range, sheer walls of stone 300m (1,000ft) high tower over the plains, where a series of catwalks and carved footpaths wander through old temples and pavilions into the silence and emptiness beyond.

SUZHOU (SOOCHOW)

For centuries **Suzhou** – rather over-enthusiastically dubbed the Venice of the East – has been famous for its canals and classical Chinese gardens, its beautiful women and the musical cadences of the local dialect. An old Chinese proverb, referring to the area's linguistic charms, claims that even an argument in Suzhou sounds sweeter than flattery in Guangzhou. Marco Polo found the inhabitants better traders than warriors, and he described the city as large and magnificent. So much silk was produced, he reported, that every citizen was clothed in it and the surplus was exported. Even today, Suzhou remains justly renowned for its silk products.

Whether you go to Suzhou from Shanghai or Nanjing, you will be moved by the wayside scenery, typical of China's 'land of fish and rice'. Sampans and scows ply the canals that divide the farmlands, where barefoot peasants in straw coolie hats squelch through the muddy rice fields. The Grand Canal is crowded with strings of barges laden with fruit and vegetables, construction materials or coal. Suzhou in fact means 'Plentiful Water'.

Suzhou's Forest of Lions Garden inspired the Qing emperors

Abundant lotus plants in the Humble Administrator's Garden

The **Grand Canal**, second only to the Great Wall as a Chinese engineering achievement, was started 2,400 years ago. By the 6th century AD it linked Suzhou and other rich farming areas of the south with the consumers of the north – most notably the emperor and his court, who appreciated receiving fresh food regardless of the season. Today the Grand Canal is little used for commerce and public transport. In fact, much of it is not navigable. But for travellers it can provide an interesting excursion. Canal trips by tourist boat often begin in Suzhou, chugging along to another enchanted city, Wuxi *(see page 176)*.

Suzhou's Gardens

But Suzhou is best known for its perfectly landscaped, classical Chinese gardens, designed to create an illusion of the universe in a small space. More than 150 were laid out, the first over 1,000 years ago, and 69 remain today. Largest of all (4 hectares/10 acres) is the **Humble Administrator's Garden** (Zhuozhengyuan; open daily 7.30am–5.30pm in summer, 8am–5pm in winter), built by a Ming dynasty mandarin not otherwise remembered for humility. As befits the City of Plentiful Water, ponds occupy the better part of the terrain. And where there are ponds there are almost bound to be artificial islands, winding bridges, gazebos, weeping willows and lotus plants – so abundant that one pavilion is called Hehua Simian Ting (You See Lotus Everywhere).

The **Forest of Lions Garden** (Shizilin; open daily 7.30am–5.30pm) dates back to 1336, its rocks from Lake Tai evoking the form and power of lions. The Qing dynasty Emperors modelled the rockeries in the Old Summer Palace in Beijing after those they saw in Suzhou's Forest of Lions.

To the west, the **Lingering Garden** (Liuyuan; open daily 7.30am–5.30pm) is a refuge of flowers, trees, courtyards and halls. Aptly named, it is a garden with many nooks and crannies, in which getting lost is a pleasure. This one, too, was built by a Ming civil servant as a place for meditation. While you linger, contemplate the 5-tonne rock shipped here 400 years ago from Lake Tai because of its inspiring shape. Nearby **West Garden** (Xiyuan; open daily 7.30am–5.30pm) originally formed a single area with Liuyuan, until the space was given to a Buddhist monastery. The temple was destroyed in the Taiping Rebellion, then rebuilt.

Silken Secrets

When the *Bombyx mori* caterpillar is ready to turn into a moth, it exudes a single fibrous strand hundreds of metres long and wraps itself into a watertight cocoon. The caterpillar is the silkworm, the strand is pure silk, and the secret of its cultivation has been known to the Chinese for 4,500 years. From the neolithic period, Chinese farmers fed silkworms on mulberry leaves and soaked the cocoons in warm water to free the silken yarn. By the 1st century AD, silk production was so prolific that an emperor was able to distribute a million rolls of silk cloth along the northern frontier to pacify marauders. Roman women craved the gossamer fabric carried to Europe along the old Silk Road. Even after a rival silk industry, based on smuggled silkworms, was set up in Syria, damasks and brocades were still exported to Europe from China, where the secret of silk manufacture was so jealously guarded that the penalty for revealing it was death by torture. Today, 10 million Chinese farmers produce more than half the world's supply of silk. The thread is wound off the cocoons almost by the kilometre, but it can take up to 1,000 cocoons to produce a single shirt.

Probably the smallest of all the Suzhou gardens, situated right in the centre of town, is the **Garden of the Master of the Nets** (Wangshiyuan; open daily 8am–4.30pm), covering half a hectare (barely an acre) and famous for its peony blossoms in spring. The garden's founder, a retired politician, claimed he had given up public life to become a fisherman. Whatever his interests, he could hardly fail to be inspired by the view from his simple study. This masterpiece of Chinese classical garden design served as the inspiration for the Astor Chinese Garden Court in New York City's Metropolitan Museum of Art.

Among Suzhou's tourist highlights, the highest is **Tiger Hill** (Huqiu; open daily 8am–6pm in summer, 8am–4pm in winter), a man-made hill built 2,500 years ago. It is rich in contrived rock formations, vegetation and waterfalls. From the summit rises a seven-level brick pagoda, **Yunyanta**. Like the one in Shanghai, it leans a bit from the vertical, although modern reinforcements

With its extensive canals, Suzhou has picturesque areas

should relieve your anxiety. Other sights worth lingering over in the old inner city include the 14th-century **Panmen Gate** (open daily 8am–5pm), where a magnificent arched bridge crosses a canal linking Suzhou to the Grand Canal and the Rui Guang Pagoda (dating from 1119).

Suzhou is also famous for its silk production. The **Suzhou Silk Museum** (open daily 9am–5.30pm) exhibits the 4,500 years of silk history in the region, and the **Museum of Suzhou Embroidery** (open daily 9am–5pm) is a working factory and sales outlet featured on many city tours. The new **Suzhou History Museum** (open daily 8.15am–4pm), designed by I.M. Pei, houses thousands of regional relics.

The chief religious site, the **Temple of Mystery** (Xuanmiaoguan; open daily 7.30am–5.30pm), includes the largest early Daoist hall in China (built in 1179) and is today surrounded by Suzhou's biggest and liveliest outdoor market.

TAISHAN

Although not well known in the West, **Taishan** is China's most celebrated peak. Everyone who was anyone in Chinese history, from Confucius to Chairman Mao, has stood on its summit. Because it was long regarded as the Sacred Mountain of the East by followers of Daoism, Taishan served as the supreme altar of worship for millions of pilgrims for over 2,000 years. It undoubtedly ranks as one of the most climbed mountains in the world. Even today it attracts large numbers of visitors, most of them from China.

Situated in Shandong Province on the railway line between Beijing and Shanghai, Taishan is only 1,545m (5,070ft) high, but it is a steep climb as it rises for views of the East China Sea. Today there are more than 20 active temples on its slopes, over 800 carved tablets and some 1,000 cliff-face inscriptions, a library of Chinese culture that is carved into the body of nature.

Tai'an, the village at Taishan's base that is some 64km (40 miles) south of Jinan, is home to the magnificent **Dai Temple**

(Daimiao; open daily 7.30am–6.30pm). This walled temple complex, which consists of more than 600 buildings, was the venue for elaborate sacrifices and provided accommodation for the emperor before his ascent of Taishan. The temple's historic treasures include a stone tablet recording the mountain's promotion to the position of 'Emperor of China', as Taishan was designated in 1011 by a Song dynasty emperor. Rarest of all is the **Qin Tablet**, carved in 209BC to commemorate the ascent of Taishan by China's first emperor, Qinshi Huangdi. The main temple also contains a statue of the God of the Mountain, Taishanwang, the Judge of the Dead. The **Hall of Heavenly Gifts** (Tiankuang Dian), one of the largest classical temple halls in China, contains a fresco more than 60m (200ft) long.

The climb to the summit of Taishan can take several hours

North of the Dai Temple, the Pilgrim's Road (Panlu) leads to the First Gate of Heaven, the entrance to the mountain. Beyond this point it is mostly massive granite steps. From the First Gate to the Middle Gate of Heaven is about 5km (3 miles), and from the Middle Gate to the top less than 3km (2 miles), but the final mile is the steepest, as the elevation rise is 1,370m (4,500ft). Anyone in a hurry can catch a bus or hire a taxi to the Middle Gate and from there take the cable car to the top.

Those who keep to the old pilgrim's path are in for a long but fascinating walk. A little way off the main path is the **Valley of the Stone Sutra** (Jing Shiyu), where 6th-century Buddhists carved the text of the Diamond Sutra into a huge, smooth block of stone. The 1,050 characters, each 50cm (20in) high, are considered a masterpiece of calligraphy. Among the other celebrated sights are the Pines of the Fifth Order of Officials (Wufaidu Song) which sheltered the emperor Qinshi Huangdi from a thunderstorm on his climb, and a final ladder of 2,000 stone steps leading to the Pavilion That Touches the Sky.

Sunrise over China's most venerated Daoist peak

On the summit there are even more treasures, but first one must negotiate the earthly delights of Tian Jie (Heaven Street), a Qing dynasty parade of shops and restaurants. The Tang dynasty **Rock Inscriptions** (Moyabei) were struck in large gold-foil characters to record Emperor Xuanzong's imperial pilgrimage in 726. The Stele Without Inscription (Wuzibei) is blank, thought to have been placed here by the First Emperor over 2,000 years earlier; everyone who reaches it must touch it for good luck.

The **Temple of the Purple Dawn** (Bixiaci) is the most revered of the shrines on the summit of Taishan. Here presides the Jade Goddess, daughter of the mountain god, who cures blindness and answers the prayers of the childless. And there are hundreds of earnest petitioners and pilgrims even today on the summit of Taishan.

At dawn, the thousands who spend the night in inns on the summit await the famous sunrise. It is precisely here that Confucius observed that the world is small and that Chairman Mao proclaimed 'the East is Red'.

TURPAN (TURFAN, TULUFAN)

The pavements of Turpan would turn to mud if it ever rained, but it almost never does. Here in the middle of the great desert in Xinjiang (Sinkiang) Autonomous Region, only 16mm (½ in) of rain ever reaches the ground in an average year.

Because of Turpan's location in the Tarim Basin – at 79m (260ft) below sea level, this is the second-deepest continental basin in the world – it's startling to discover here a sizeable city where houses are supplied with electricity and running water and shady trees line the streets. It's an amazing oasis, a bastion of civilisation in a climate as cruel as any on earth.

Turpan's secret is underground water, utilised today as it has been for thousands of years by a system of interconnecting wells *(karez)* that use gravity to relay water from the Heavenly Mountains (Tianshan) underground to the oasis. (If the aqueduct were above ground, the water would almost all be lost through evaporation.) Over the whole region, these water tunnels, all dug by hand, stretch for perhaps 3,000km (more than 1,800 miles), with some individual tunnels running as far as 40km (25 miles).

Thanks to the wells, Turpan grows cotton, melons and grapes of great sweetness and renown. And the surrounding desert is kept at bay by bountifully irrigated stands of elm, poplar and palm trees. The *karez* is an engineering feat on a par with that of the Grand Canal, and an exhibition centre at one well site allows visitors to enter several of these hand-dug wells for a close-up view.

The climatic conditions of China's 'oven' are nevertheless hostile to humans. In the summer, when the temperature

A Uighur family on the road to Turpan market

exceeds 40°C (104°F) for days at a time, the locals take refuge in cellars until the night breeze comes up. In winter it's a different story altogether, with the mercury plummeting, and residents dressing for the big chill – the men in their long underwear and the women in thick brown stockings and gaily coloured headscarves.

Turpan is about 200km (125 miles) southeast of Urumqi, the regional capital *(see page 169)*. It's so dry and (except for winter) hot in the oasis that tourists are advised to drink as much tea or juice as possible to prevent dehydration. Laundry on washing lines dries in a matter of minutes rather than hours or days.

The Emin Minaret: more Afghan than Chinese in architectural style

Two thousand years ago, the Silk Road traders stopped in Turpan to find water and rest. The **bazaar** of today might give you the impression that little has changed. There are outdoor butcher shops, cobblers, dentists and a shooting gallery, plus merchants selling medicinal herbs, embroidered skullcaps and tobacco by the pocketful. Makeshift restaurants dish up spicy kebabs and the bread called *nang*. The customers, mostly of the Uighur nationality – Uighurs make up 80 percent of Turpan's residents – give this Silk Road oasis a most un-Chinese atmosphere.

Minarets outnumber pagodas here, and just east of the city is **Emin Minaret** (Sugong Ta; open daily 8am–8pm) a stunning 44-m (144-ft) tower of clay brick that was erected in 1778. The attached white stone mosque, with its plain interior, is the largest in the region and can hold up to 3,000 worshippers. It is used only during important Muslim festivals, although a square for vendors was recently built here.

Excursions from Turpan

The most remarkable sites in the area are the ruins of two ancient desert capitals. The city of **Jiaohe** (open daily dawn–dusk), 10km (6 miles) west of Turpan, was founded in the 2nd century BC and laid out in a grid. Destroyed at the end of the 14th century, its sand and brick still preserve the haunting outlines of a great city that stretched for a mile, with a Buddhist temple and headless statues at the centre. There are remains of underground dwellings, which offered protection from the elements.

> Several joint Chinese-Japanese expeditions to the Xinjiang region in western China have uncovered important dinosaur fossil fields, especially from the Jurassic era.

Gaochang (open daily dawn–dusk), a second ancient city, 46km (29 miles) east of Turpan, has an imposing city wall with a perimeter of 5km (3 miles). Gaochang reached its prime during the Tang dynasty, when it became a capital of China's western territories. During its heyday, it had 30,000 inhabitants and more than 3,000 monks in over 40 Buddhist monasteries. When Islam overtook Buddhism here in the 13th century, Gaochang was abandoned. Visitors today usually hire a Uighur donkey cart for a tour of the earthen remains.

A few miles from Gaochang is the royal **Astana Cemetery** (Astana-Karakhoja Mu; open daily dawn–dusk), a burial ground for Gaochang's dead, with well over 500 tombs, the oldest dating from AD273. The cemetery was discovered by accident in 1972. Because of the almost total lack of moisture, the murals in the tombs have retained their original lively colours – and many of the corpses haven't aged much either. Visitors can enter several of the underground burial chambers, including one where a couple buried together 12 centuries ago lie side by side, their hair and fingernails grown long in death.

Northeast of Turpan, the road skirts the **Flaming Mountains** (Kizilatak in Uighur, Huoyanshan in Chinese). Facing south, the slopes attract and store the sun's heat – temperatures here have reached as high as 55°C (131°F). On a sheer cliff in a gorge in these mountains, perch the Bezeklik Thousand Buddha Caves, with carvings and frescoes dating from the 5th century. Unfortunately, these beautiful grottoes have been largely emptied by rival religious groups and by archaeological looters from the West. The 40 painted walls and ceilings that remain have almost faded into the grey dust of the engulfing desert.

URUMQI (WULUMUQI)

In Mongolian, Urumqi means 'Fine Pasture'. In Uighur, it's spelled with umlauts: Ürümqi. The Chinese make four syllables of it. However you read or write it, Urumqi sounds remote and exotic. Remote it certainly is – the most distant major city in the

A parched, empty highway of the Western Desert

world from any ocean or saltwater sea. Exotic? In fact, Urumqi has an exotic population of minority and nomadic peoples, but it has been developed by the Han Chinese into a modern industrial city. And the Han Chinese (mostly recent 'economic' migrants) make up 75 percent of its 3 million residents.

Urumqi is the capital of the Xinjiang Uighur Autonomous Region, which covers one-sixth of China. It borders Afghanistan, Pakistan, India, Tajikistan, Kyrgyzstan, Kazakhstan and Mongolia on the old Silk Road route through Central Asia, and more than half of the province's population belongs to minority groups, led by the Uighurs. The greatest attractions lie well outside the city, in scenic highlands where nomads still reign.

Urumqi, which lies 900m (2,950ft) above sea level, is the most modern and most Chinese city on the Silk Road. City-centre avenues are broad and tree-lined, there are dozens of mosques, and the street markets provide splashes of colour. At the largest covered market, the **Erdaoqiao Bazaar**, vendors sell handmade goods from boots to carpets, and herds of sheep and donkey carts ply the alleyways. The most irresistible items are edible: kebabs, homemade noodles and round flatbreads, cooked on-the-spot over coal fires.

Amid the modern high-rise buildings and the mosques in Urumqi are a number of buildings dating from the time of the Soviet presence and influence. They are conspicuous for their sterile exteriors.

The **Xinjiang Museum** (Xinjiang Bowuguan; open Tues–Sun 10.30am–1pm and 4–8pm in summer, 10.30am–1pm and 3.30–7.30pm in winter), with explanatory cards in English, Chinese and Uighur, contains Silk Road coins, earrings, tiles, silks and a fascinating collection of mummies, embalmed as long ago as the 13th century BC. There are also life-sized models of the houses and tools of the most important nationalities in the region, and some 3,000-year-old corpses of European and Mongolian ancestry. The museum shops carry the main

The sumptuous interior of a nomadic Kazakh family's *yurt*

local products: Persian-style carpets, ornate skullcaps, deadly looking knives in bronze scabbards (which many of the local people carry), stringed instruments and white jade.

Two sites with Chinese characteristics on the Urumqi River, **Red Hill** (Hongshan) – topped by the 18th-century Zhenglong Pagoda – and **Hongshan Park**, on the west bank, are favourite leisure and picnic grounds for the locals.

Around Urumqi

In the **Southern Mountains** (Nanshan), 74km (46 miles) south of Urumqi, the Kazakhs move their families on horseback and set up their *yurts* on the high pastures to graze their sheep. At the end of the road, near an Alpine waterfall, the Kazakhs, who once rode with Genghis and Kublai Khan across these grasslands, open their village to visitors and in July stage a six-day summer fair *(nadam)* with horse races and wrestling.

A more famous scenic spot is **Heavenly Lake** (Tianchi), 120km (75 miles) east of Urumqi, one of the prettiest mountain lakes in the world. It is surrounded by *yurts*, grazing sheep and

A cruise boat moored at Wuhan

snowy peaks, capped by Mt Bogda, with an elevation of 5,444m (17,864ft). In this alluring high-country Shangri-La, the Kazakhs are happy to share their food, shelter and horses with paying guests who want to ride the lake rim or spend the night in a *yurt*. The road between Urumqi and the lake is newly built and passes through some lovely scenery.

WUHAN

A lively industrial and intellectual centre, Wuhan is nearly equidistant between Beijing and Guangzhou, and between Shanghai and Chongqing. Its setting at the confluence of the Yangzi and Han rivers has made it an important traffic junction. Here, the wail of riverboat foghorns mingles with train whistles on the nation's main north–south railway. Cruises along the Yangzi from Wuhan to Chongqing, or vice versa, are among China's most exciting boat trips *(see page 81)*.

The story of Wuhan has always been anchored in the vital, muddy Yangzi. So wide and treacherous is the river that, before the construction of the great concrete and steel bridge of Wuhan (the first to cross the Yangzi) in 1957, all communications depended on the ferries, which were often hampered by fog or flood. Now the two-tiered **Yangzi River Bridge** (Changjiang Daqiao) is proudly shown to tourists as a triumph of the new China. So are the dykes, so tall they cut off the view of the river from the embankment. But the Yangzi's rages can't always be contained. In 1983 Wuhan was flooded in spite of monumental preparations, and the great floods of 1998 (the worst in 54 years) again pushed Wuhan to the brink.

Wuhan is actually a modern, composite name for three historic, contiguous cities: Wuchang, Hankou and Hanyang. Wuchang, the oldest, is bountifully supplied with parklands. Hankou, on the opposite bank of the Yangzi, was opened to foreign development in the 19th century as a Treaty Port; at high tide 10,000-tonne ships can reach Hankou's harbour from the sea, some 1,500km (1,000 miles) away. Hanyang, separated from Hankou by the Han River (requiring another, less heroic bridge), is more typically Chinese.

After the Opium Wars, Hankou was carved up into separate British, French, German, Japanese and Russian zones of influence. Along Zhong-shan Avenue, near the Yangzi ferry terminals, some of the old European-style buildings still remain. The municipal office buildings on the embankment, administering a city which has now grown

Chang Jiang, the Chinese name for the Yangzi, means Long River – appropriately enough for, at 6,300km (3,915 miles), it's the longest river in China and the third longest in the world.

well beyond 4 million, are cast in the German mould.

But Wuhan, the capital of Hubei Province, also has a significant revolutionary history. The rebellion of October 1911, which was inspired by Dr Sun Yat-sen, began in Wuchang, and Hankou suffered heavy damage in the fighting. The Central Peasant Movement Institute, where communist activists were trained in the 1920s, was established in Wuchang. Mao Zedong taught

here, and his legacy is strong at several tourist attractions, including a villa (Mao Zedong Bieshu; open daily 8am–5pm) where he often spent holidays and several displays at the provincial museum.

Wuhan Sights

The **Hubei Provincial Museum** (Hubeisheng Bowuguan; open daily 9am–4pm) owes its excellence to the chance discovery in 1978 of the tomb of the Marquis Yi of the State of Zeng. Located 108km (67 miles) northwest of Wuhan,

The Yangzi above Wuhan

the grave yielded enough treasure to furnish several museums. About 1,000 items – a mere 15 percent of the total hoard – are now on display here. When Yi died in 433BC, he was greatly mourned. He was buried with his dog and 21 sacrificed women, as well as tributes ranging from bronze wine vessels to enough musical instruments for an orchestra. The finest musical exhibit in the collection is a set of 65 intricately decorated bronze bells (*bianzhong*), still possessing perfect pitch and tone. It has proved impossible to replicate the casting methods used, and the bells have been played only twice. However, modern duplicates have been made, and visitors can hear a tape recording, and occasional concerts featuring these interpreting both Chinese and Western music; they sound like a cross between a glockenspiel and a modern carillon.

The museum looks out on to **East Lake** (Dong Hu; open daily 24 hours), vaunted as the largest lake in any municipal park in China, with 33 sq km (nearly 13 sq miles) of invitingly clear water. Boating, swimming and fishing are popular here. Of course, no Chinese lake would be complete without its artificial islands, causeways and pavilions, several of which serve as tea-houses festooned with peach and plum blossoms, orchids or osmanthus, depending on the season.

Hanyang's main religious landmark, **Gui Yuan Temple** (Guiyuan Chansi; open daily 8am–5pm), sprawls among pines and cypresses. Built in the 17th century, it was the only one of Wuhan's 20 or more Buddhist temples spared by rampaging Red Guards during the Cultural Revolution (1966–76). The Hall of Five Hundred Disciples is a fascinating gallery of statues. Grinning, yawning, frowning, meditating and leering, each one is different.

The Northern Song dynasty **Ancient Lute Terrace** (Guqintai; open daily 7.30am–4pm) commemorates a 2,500-year-old legend of the deep friendship between a lute-playing mandarin in Chu kingdom, named Yu Boya, and a music-loving woodcutter. Amateur musicians hold forth in the teahouse here, a favourite meeting place of local pensioners.

The Grandest of Canals

The boats and barges that throng the Grand Canal at Wuxi recall the days when this great waterway was China's main north–south artery. For more than 2,000 years successive dynasties linked lakes and rivers to create a single canal, 40 paces wide, that went from Hangzhou, across the Yangzi and Yellow rivers, to the old capital Chang'an (now Xi'an) and on to Beijing. Paved roads built along each bank were shaded by elms and willows. To celebrate the extension of the canal in 610, the emperor sailed along it in his four-decked imperial barge, escorted by a flotilla of dragon boats and followed by a retinue of eunuchs, concubines and officials. In its heyday, some 15,000 junks, sampans and barges plied the water highway, carrying grain, timber, salt, fish, cloth, pottery and luxury goods. With the advent of the railways and coastal steamers, the canal lost its importance. Crops were often grown and houses built in the old canal bed. But today the Grand Canal is being restored and used once again as a means of transport as well as to water the rice fields.

Picturesque Lake Tai is celebrated in Chinese legend

Across the 1.5-km (1-mile) Yangzi River Bridge in Wuchang is the **Yellow Crane Tower** (Huanghelou; open daily 8am–6pm in summer, 8am–5.30pm in winter), based on another legend. First built in AD223, the wooden structure burnt down and was reconstructed several times. In 1981, the latest rebuilding project got under way about 1km (½ mile) from the original site. The design and decor of the new tower are based on paintings from the Yuan and Ming dynasties and a model of the bridge as it existed in the Qing dynasty.

WUXI

This appealing town really does deserve a more poetic name. Wuxi means 'no more tin', a reference to the depletion, a couple of thousand years ago, of the local mines. Wuxi is an industrial and marketing centre with a population of more than 4 million in the 'land of fish and rice', a fertile semitropical region. It lies 128km (80 miles) northwest of Shanghai, close enough for a day trip. Canals and rivers crisscross the city, and the **Grand Canal**, Wuxi's prime historic attraction, flows right through the centre of town from Lake Tai, Wuxi's prime scenic attraction.

Even a short boat ride through the city on the Grand Canal produces unforgettable sights and photos. Many people line the bridges (each of a different design) to wave. Human-propelled ferryboats scurry out of the way as long trains of barges, their decks heaped up with onions, reeds or bricks, labour past. The riverside dwellers, who live in quaint whitewashed houses, wash their clothes in the canal. You might see a fisherman assigning his captive cormorants to dive, their gullets collared to stop them from eating the catch.

The Grand Canal project, begun 2,400 years ago, created an inland waterway stretching 1,794km (1,113 miles) from Beijing to Hangzhou. Canal excursions organised for foreign tourists range from a half-day tour to a seven-day cruise that takes in Suzhou, Wuxi, Changzhou and Zhenjiang, in addition to the Yangzi River port of Yangzhou.

Lake Tai

Lake Tai (Taihu), a vast freshwater expanse with 72 islets, is the most celebrated lake in Chinese legend. **Turtle Head Island** (Yuantouzhu; open daily 6am–5pm) is actually a peninsula at the edge of Lake Tai, a sanctuary of trees, flowers, bridges and lake-viewing pavilions that began as a garden in 1918. But more than any specific landfall, the lake is a spectacle on its own, with its fleet of fishing junks and roving sampans. Visitors can easily take to the waters aboard the public ferries (daily 8.15am– 5.50pm) to **Three Hills Island** (Sanshandao). Largely an amusement park situated in the middle of the lake, Three Hills (known locally as Xiandao or 'Fairy Island') contains a new four-tiered temple with the modern statue of an ancient emperor, providing an enchanting view of Lake Tai from the top. (Ferries run every day from 8.15am–5.50pm.)

Xihui Park in Wuxi

To underline the monumental character of Lake Tai in legend and in nature, the world's largest standing statue of Buddha was unveiled in 1997 at Lingshan on the lake shore 18km (11 miles) west of Wuxi. **Lingshan Dafo** (open daily 6.30am–6pm) to give the giant its Chinese name, is fashioned from bronze plates, weighs 700 tonnes and stands 73m (240ft) tall.

Wuxi is also home to two classic gardens. **Li Garden** (Liyuan; open daily 6.30am–7.30pm) has arched bridges, gaudy pavilions, open walkways, fish ponds, a miniature pagoda and a covered walkway with 89 view-framing windows. The more resplendent **Jichang Garden** (Jichangyuan; open daily 7am–dusk), established in 1520, is a Suzhou-style private garden much admired by Emperor Qianlong, who constructed a similar garden in Beijing's Summer Palace in 1750.

Jichang Garden is contained within **Xihui Park** (open daily 5am–dusk) on the Grand Canal, site of the seven-tiered Ming dynasty Dragon Light Pagoda (Longguang) and a spring tulip

Dawn in Xiamen, officially China's cleanest city

festival with flowers imported from Holland. The park also contains **Erquan Spring**, source of some of the world's best water for tea brewing, according to the *Classic of Tea* (Chajing), written by the scholar Luyu. But it is two modern attractions that lure most Chinese visitors: the first is the **cable-car** ride (daily 8.30am–5pm) that connects Xishan Hill with Huishan, the other large hill visible from Wuxi. On clear days, the ride affords soaring views of the city and lake; beware of vertigo though, as the trip is remarkably high and long.

> **Among Lake Tai's attractions are Tang City, Three Kingdoms City and Water Margins City – all originally built as sets for TV series in the 1980s and '90s, and now offering live daily scenes from the shows.**

Even more notable is the tunnel that cuts right through the middle of Xishan. The **Dragon Light Cave** echoes with the digital whistles and roars of a hundred scattered robotic creatures, all lurking in dark rooms off an intimidatingly long corridor. Walk from end to end, and marvel at surreal, 2-m (6-ft) singing carrots; fend off twitching Teenage Mutant Ninja Turtles, gasping dinosaurs and motionless penguins; and most importantly, stay away from the huge, whistling and highly dangerous fish-eating insects.

XIAMEN (AMOY)

China's cleanest major city (according to an official poll) and one of its most charming, **Xiamen** is a port city located in Fujian Province, hardly a heartbeat from Taiwan across the East China Sea. A prosperous place owing to its close connections with overseas Chinese investors (many of whom emigrated from the area), Xiamen has wisely spared much of its old town and harbour from the bulldozers of progress.

From the busy harbour square, overlooked by the balconies of the venerable Lujiang Hotel, you can stroll into old-town areas along Zhongshan Road, past dozens of antiques shop-houses and cafés. Or you can head south along Minzu Road and take in the life of the fishing boats and warehouses on the quays.

If you walk long enough (or hail a taxi), you end up at **Nanputuo Temple** (open daily sunrise–sunset), nestled in the hillside on the east shore of the harbour. This Buddhist complex is in immaculate condition, its marble a gleaming white. Locals are always on hand, burning incense and praying for good fortune. The rocky cliffs behind the temple make for fine hiking and picnicking.

South of the temple and past **Xiamen University** (founded in 1921 by a local who made good in Singapore) is the **Huli Mountain Cannon Platform**. In 1921 the Germans placed their artillery here to defend the colonial port of Amoy, as Xiamen was known to Westerners. From here, if you look across the Formosa Strait on a sunny day, you can make out the disputed islands of Mazu and Jinmen. Once known to Western politicians as 'Matsu' and 'Quemoy', these islands figured in the Nixon-Kennedy presidential debates of 1960. Today, the 'cold war' between China and Taiwan, often waged with loudspeakers and leaflet bombardments across the Formosa Strait, appears to be over, and the two islands have been opened to tourism by Taiwan.

Gulangyu

Xiamen's chief pleasure for any visitor is **Gulangyu**, a small island in the harbour that was once the home to foreign colonials. Passenger ferries connect downtown Xiamen to the island. Gulangyu has banned automotive vehicles and is a pedestrian's island – not even bicycles are allowed here. The terrain is hilly, with twisting cobblestone streets forming a compact maze, but you're always within sight of the shoreline. The lanes are full of villas and grand European buildings. Beginning in 1842, Western traders allowed in after the Opium Wars built Gulangyu into a virtual European town, with their own schools, churches and hospitals. The British Embassy still stands on a hill above the ferry landing, and beyond it the Roman Catholic church, completed in 1882 and still in use. The Sanyi Protestant church, built by the British in 1904, is also active. These days, the colonial villas are occupied by local Chinese. The ripe gardens give Gulangyu a lazy, tropical atmosphere reminiscent of Macau or Malacca.

A statue of the patron saint of Xiamen, Koxinga (Zheng Chenggong), stands on the tip of the island. A warrior in flowing robes, he expelled the Dutch from Taiwan in the 17th century. Not far from Koxinga's heroic image are the guesthouse villas and sandy beaches where locals relax and sometimes even take a dip. Above the beaches is the island's most famous garden, **Shuzhuang** (open daily 8.30am–5pm), built in 1913 by a wealthy Taiwanese merchant and admired for its pond and rock design: 'a garden in the sea, a sea in the garden'.

The best views are from the towering **Sunlight Rock** (Riguangyan) in Yanping Park, the highest point on Gulangyu and well worth the climb. From here, you can see across the long harbour to downtown Xiamen. And of course you can see

Some Xi'an streets have hardly changed in centuries

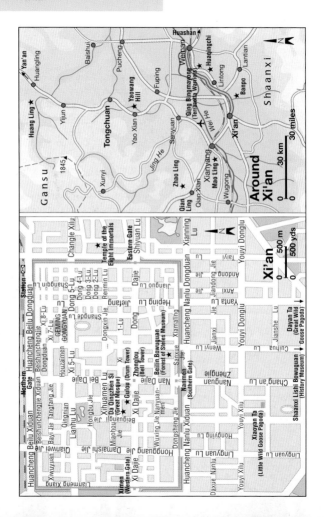

Around Xi'an

Huashan ★
Weinan
Huayinchi
Lintong
Banpo ★
Lantian
Qing Bingmayong (Terracotta Warriors) ★
Xi'an
Wei He
Baishui
Pucheng
Fuping
Huangling
Yan'an
Yichun
Huang Ling ★
Yaowang Hill ★
Tongchuan
Yao Xian
Sanyuan
Shaanxi
Jing He
Xunyi
1845 ▲
Gansu
Zhao Ling ★
Xianyang
Mao Ling ★
Wugong
Qian Xian
Qian Ling ★

N
0   30 km
0   30 miles

Xi'an

N
0   500 m
0   500 yds

Station
Northern Gate
Eastern Gate
Temple of the Eight Immortals
Changle Xilu
Shiyuan Lu
Xianning Lu

Huancheng Beilu Dongduan
Beishunchengjie Dongduan
Shangqin Lu
Dong 5-Lu
Dong 4-Lu
Dong 3-Lu
Dong 2-Lu
Renmin Lu
Dong Dajie
Jiefang Lu
Heping Lu
Jianguo Lu
Youyi Donglu

GEMING GONGYUAN
Xi 8-Lu
Xi 7-Lu
Shangde Lu
Dongxin Jie
Dong
1-Lu
Xiamating
Sanxue
Taiyi Lu
Jiandong Jie
Anxi
Anjong Lu

Huancheng Beilu Xiduan
Beishunchengjie Xiduan
Dongduan
Houzaimen
Xihuamen Lu
Bei Dajie
Xi
Zhonglou (Bell Tower)
Berlin Bowuguan (Forest of Steles Museum)
Huancheng Nanlu Dongduan
Yanta Lu
Jianxi

Xi 5-Lu
Qingnian
Bayi Jie
Lianhu Lu
Da Qingzhen Si (Great Mosque)
Gulou (Drum Tower)
Nan Dajie
Xianning Lu
Wenyi Lu
Cuihua Lu
Dayan Ta (Great Wild Goose Pagoda)

Hongbu Jie
Hongfu Jie
Miaohou Jie
Xihuamen Lu
Beiguangjie Jie
Nanmen (Southern Gate)
Nanyuanmen
Nanguan Zhengjie
Chang'an Lu
Shaanxi Lishi Bowuguan (History Museum)
Jianshe Lu

Qianwei Jie
Xiwuyuan
Bayi Jie Tangfang Jie
Damashi Jie
Hongguang Jie
Xi Dajie
Wuxing Jie
Dongsheng Jie
Huancheng Nanlu Xiduan
Youyi Xilu
Hongying Lu
Lingyuan Lu
Youyi Donglu

Ximen (Western Gate)
Xi Dajie
Liamgeng Xiang
Daxue Nanlu
Youyi Xilu
Xiaoyan Ta (Little Wild Goose Pagoda)

Gulangyu itself, a dense sea garden of flowers, red-tiled villas and tiny seafood cafés – a bright home to just 12,000 residents. (By comparison, the city of Xiamen has over 600,000 citizens and is a rampaging metropolis.)

The **Xiamen Museum**, housed in Gulangyu's most striking red-domed building, contains a sprinkling of different exhibits on its four floors, including printing presses, Tang dynasty porcelains, wooden rifles, assorted gifts from sister cities around the world, and photographs of the island's dazzling colonial architecture.

XI'AN

When ancient Beijing was just a remote trading post, **Xi'an** was the capital of the Middle Kingdom and the largest city in the world. Palaces, pavilions and pagodas crowned the skyline. Artists and poets (and, of course, cooks) catered for the most demanding imperial tastes. And since this was the starting point of the Silk Road, the most adventurous of foreigners congregated here.

The centre of Xi'an still retains its historical layout from the Tang dynasty, with roads laid out in a classical Chinese grid pattern, running due north–south or east–west, and meeting at right-angles.

Having made history over several thousand years, the city of today is more populous than ever (at 6 million residents) and proud of its leafy new avenues, modern factories and housing projects. But there's no avoiding the past in this treasure trove of Chinese civilisation. Xi'an and its surrounding countryside preserve the glories of eleven dynasties, and it is as a storehouse of China's Qin, Han and Tang dynasty treasures that Xi'an has reached the top ranks of international tourism.

On the way to any of Xi'an's archaeological sites, you get a good look at the wind-whipped landscape of the Wei River valley. Militarily and economically strategic since prehistoric times, the area comprises fertile cotton and wheat fields, fallow plains and bizarre terraces of grey clay dotted with caves that provide housing even to this day.

As the rapidly modernising capital of Shaanxi Province, Xi'an can look back almost with detachment on its regal past. During the first Zhou dynasty (which ended in 770BC), several places in the Xi'an district served as capitals. In the 3rd century BC, the Qin settled just northwest of Xi'an, in Xianyang. When the Han took over, in 206BC, a grandiose new capital called Chang'an ('Everlasting Peace') rose just north of Xi'an. Imperial splendour returned to the region under the Sui (AD581–618) when a capital known as Daxing ('Great Prosperity') was established on the site of Xi'an. The Tang emperors who followed greatly enlarged and beautified the city, again naming it Chang'an.

The golden age of Xi'an (as Chang'an) ended more than 1,000 years ago, when the Tang succumbed to rebellion and anarchy. The city sank into provinciality, even though impres-

Some of the massive Ming dynasty city wall has been restored

sive new city walls and official buildings were constructed in the 14th century. These features of the Ming era – almost modern by Xi'an standards – are the first to catch the eye.

Sightseeing in Xi'an

The rectangular Ming dynasty city wall of Xi'an is 14.5km (almost 9 miles) around and so thick that two-way chariot traffic could travel the roadway on top. Major renovations have restored some of the ramparts, guard towers and city moat. Gardens and parks complement these massive fortifications, the last major city walls standing intact in China.

In the centre of the walled city are several monuments from the Ming dynasty. The **Bell Tower** (Zhonglou; open daily 8am–7pm) is another of those lofty wooden buildings ingeniously constructed without the use of nails. Three tiers of elegant roofs rise from a solid brick pedestal at the centre of the city, forming one of the emblems of Xi'an.

The **Drum Tower** (Gulou; open daily 8am–7pm), a similar building across a new public square and shopping mall, dates from 1370 and is also open to tourists. Among the most popular new tourist treats are the bell-striking and drum-beating ceremonies carried out daily by 'warriors' to the sound of re-creations of Tang dynasty music. The drum is sounded in its tower 21 times at sunrise; the bell is sounded in its tower 21 times at sunset.

Religious Sites

Just around the corner and up a curving alleyway of vendors, the **Great Mosque** (Daqingzhensi; open daily 8am–8pm) traces its history to AD742. The serene and spacious complex consists of gardens, temples and pavilions, largely in the Chinese style. The side galleries contain beautifully carved furniture and screens. The triple-eaved Introspection Tower (Shengxin) is a minaret from which many of Xi'an's sizeable Muslim minority, including descendants of Silk Road travellers, are called to prayer. The prayer hall holds over 1,000.

Xi'an's once-glorious temples were devastated during the Cultural Revolution (1966–76), but restorations have led to the reopening of the **Lama Temple** (Guangrensi), founded in 1705; **Wolongsi**, an ancient Zen Buddhist temple; **Dongyuemiao**, a Daoist temple to the mountain god of Taishan; and the **Temple of the Eight Immortals** (Baxianan; open daily 8am–5pm), which is the most active of the city's religious shrines at the current time and has an open-air market.

Museums

A clay tiger in traditional style, in the Forest of Steles Museum

Xi'an has a number of fine museums. The **Shaanxi History Museum** (Shaanxi Lishi Bowuguan; open winter and spring 9am–4.30pm, summer and autumn 8.30am–5.30pm), south of the city wall, is the most extensive. With a collection rivalled only by the exhibits in the Shanghai Museum *(see page 150)*, the museum is housed in a modern building with Tang design features. The museum presents intelligently arranged pieces that largely focus on the Han, Qin and Tang dynasties. Also on display are some magnificent Shang bronzes and some excellent ceramics, including *sancai* (three colour) pieces from the Tang dynasty, as well as a rare tiger-shaped tally patterned with archaic Chinese characters.

Also of great interest is the **Forest of Steles Museum** (Beilin Bowuguan; open daily 8am–6pm), located in the former Confucius Temple. This library of inscribed stone slabs, including a complete edition of the Confucian classics (carved in AD837), documents the history of Chinese culture and calligraphy. The Nestorian Stele records another history altogether, that of Christianity in China from 635 to 781. The art of calligraphy is exalted in this museum as nowhere else. The street leading to the old museum along the southern city wall, Shuyuanmen, has been restored and offers a fine collection of traditional art and calligraphy shops.

Pagodas

When the **Big Wild Goose Pagoda** (Dayanta; open daily 8am–6.30pm) was built in AD652 during the Tang dynasty, it stood well within the walled city. But Xi'an has since shrunk in size, and now the seven-tiered brick pagoda rises in the middle of farming country to the south of the urban area. Grass grows from the pagoda's roofs. The Big Wild Goose Pagoda was built to house precious Buddhist texts brought back from India by Xi'an's most celebrated pilgrim, an intrepid scholar named Xuanzang. Having survived years of sandstorms and blizzards, demons and dragons, Xuanzang was feted on his return to the capital in 645. He spent the next two decades translating his stack of holy books from Sanskrit to Chinese.

Though it's shorter, slimmer and slightly newer than the Big Wild Goose Pagoda, the **Small Wild Goose Pagoda** (Xiaoyanta; open daily 8am–6.30pm), built in 707, has more tiers: 13 at the moment. When it was built, it had 15 tiers, but the top came tumbling down in a Ming-era earthquake. Both these exquisite Tang dynasty towers (the finest of their kind in China) can be climbed, yielding interesting views of the walled city and beyond.

Excursions from Xi'an

The oldest of the region's archaeological wonders are found in a museum erected on the very site where they were discovered. This is at the Stone-Age site of **Banpo** (open daily 8am–6.30pm), 10km (6 miles) east of Xi'an. Six thousand years ago a village, evidently thriving, occupied this farmland, but traces of habitation came to light only in the 1950s, when workmen were digging the foundations for a new factory.

You have to climb a flight of stairs to reach the covered excavation. From a series of walkways you look down on the outlines of houses, ovens, storage areas and graves. You can follow the evolution of dwellings in China from round structures to rectangular houses with slanting roofs, the prototypes for today's typical Chinese abode. Also on display in the **Banpo Museum** (Banpo Bowuguan) are some of the objects found in the course of excavations: axes, fishhooks and utilitarian pots, as well as artistically decorated ceramics and, most dramatically, the skeletons of these ancient villagers.

Terracotta Warriors

China's greatest archaeological attraction, the **terracotta warriors of the Qin dynasty Army**, stand in battle formation about 30km (18 miles) east of Xi'an in the complex known as the **Museum of the Terracotta Warriors and Horses** (Qinshihuang Bingmayong Bowuguan; open daily 8am–5.30pm). The life-sized (and slightly larger) infantrymen, archers, officers and their horses symbolically guard the tomb of the first Qin emperor.

Well before his eventual death in 210BC, Qinshi Huangdi conscripted hundreds of thousands of his subjects to construct a suitably impressive tomb. It is said that the workers and supervisors involved in its de-

Each of the thousands of terracotta warriors has individual features

sign and construction were buried alive within the tomb. The novel idea of guarding it with thousands of pottery soldiers was revealed by accident in 1974, when local peasants digging a well created a worldwide sensation. Today the underground army of terracotta warriors is one of the true highlights of any visit to China.

What is believed to be the main tomb of the emperor is situated about 1.5km (1 mile) to the west of the terracotta soldiers. According to historical stories, a splendid necropolis apparently depicting the whole of China in miniature is centred beneath the 47-m (154-ft) high mound. The whole burial site is reputed to cover 56 sq km (22 sq miles). Some speculation has it that

the emperor was so superstitious and fearful that he had the necropolis built as a decoy and is, in fact, buried somewhere else. However, in order to open up the entire necropolis, 12 villages and about half a dozen factories in the area would have to be relocated.

An arched structure resembling an aircraft hangar has been built to protect the exposed soldiers and horses in Vault 1 from the weather. Walkways permit tourists a bird's-eye survey of the site, revealing the deployment of the troops, 6,000 of them reassembled and back in their original ranks. Each warrior is an individual, with his own headdress, moustache or beard and unique expression. The eager, graceful horses also have distinctive traits. The small museum in the courtyard entrance to Vault 1 contains warriors, their steeds and one of the two half-life-sized solid bronze chariots found near the First Emperor's burial mound in 1980.

Vault 2, discovered in 1976 and opened in 1994, is an excavation in progress. It contains the imperial cavalry: 900 soldiers, 116 saddled horses and 356 horses hitched to 89 chariots. Vault 3, the smallest so far opened to the public, is a command post with 68 officers in war robes.

The terracotta warriors were originally brightly coloured, with rosy cheeks and painted uniforms. Two of the archers in Vault 2 retain some of their brilliance.

Hot Springs

History and natural beauty mingle easily at **Huaqing Hot Springs** (Huaqingchi; open daily 8am–7pm), a popular side trip for tourists on the way to or from the terracotta warriors excavations. The spa's hot, mineral-rich waters and its situation on **Black Horse Mountain** (Lishan) attracted a series of royal patrons as far back as the 8th century BC. The emperors and their retinue required suitable accommodation, so the place was provided with delightful pavilions, pools and gardens.

There is one attraction in particular that draws crowds of eager Chinese tourists: the large, mosaic-bottomed Oval Tub

Within the Qianling Tombs, handmaidens wait on princess Yong Tai

used by Lady Yangguifei, favourite concubine of the Tang Emperor Xuanzong (who reigned AD712–756). Lady Yang was a famous beauty, as a portrait, hanging in her former dressing room, attests. It is said that women who wash their face in the basin will look 10 years younger. Although she was dear to the emperor, Lady Yang's extravagances and intrigues angered courtiers. When mutinous troops demanded her head, the intimidated emperor acceded to save his throne. After she was taken away and strangled, the grief-stricken emperor wept and then abdicated. The sad story is the subject of many classic poems.

Qianling Tombs

Xi'an is surrounded by hundreds of huge earthen mounds – the largely unopened tombs of emperors and their courts. The tombs of notables of the Tang dynasty, dug into a mountainside (Liangshan) about 80km (50 miles) northwest of Xi'an, provide an intriguing look at what lies buried around the old capital and at the level of art and culture reached in China during the 7th,

8th and 9th centuries. Most of the tombs that are open to the public can be visited daily 8am–6pm.

Several tombs here contain exquisite murals. The famous set of frescoes in the **tomb of Prince Zhanghuai** (who died in 684AD) depicts an animated polo match, a hunting expedition, a reception for foreign diplomats and (most movingly) a scene in a court cloister with a young concubine looking longingly at a bird in flight. A tomb with a steeply inclined entrance, that of **Princess Yong Tai**, has a mural which is full of intriguing details depicting the court maidens attending the princess (who was to die at the age of 17 in 701AD). These tombs have also yielded brightly coloured ceramic figurines, fine stone carvings and large memorial tablets.

The principal tomb belongs to the third Tang emperor, **Gaozong**, and to his ambitious widow, Wuzetian, who had herself promoted to the rank of empress in 691 – the only woman to hold such power in Chinese history. Gigantic stone sculptures of animals, birds, generals and (now headless) ambassadors line the Royal Way to this tomb, but its entrance remains sealed. The peasants of the time are said to have knocked off the ambassadors' heads during a famine because they believed the foreigners were the cause of their hardship. The ostentation of the exterior hints at what might lie within.

OTHER ATTRACTIONS

The following cities and sights are among the additional attractions that might be included on tours and itineraries.

Baotou, Inner Mongolia

Founded in the 5th century, this 'steel city on the prairie' has become the biggest industrial centre of Inner Mongolia. Two Tibetan-style pagodas and a steam locomotive museum figure prominently on the sparse sightseeing agenda. Baotou has few historic sights of its own but serves as a starting-off point for trips to the dazzling dunes of Singing Sands Gorge, the serene temples of Wudangzhao Monastery, or the Mongolian-style mau-

Baotou, in Inner Mongolia, has two Tibetan-style pagodas

soleum (Chengji Sihan Lingyuan) supposedly containing the remains of Ghenghis Khan, near the settlement of Dongsheng.

Beihai, Guangxi Province

This tropical port in southwest China has one of the country's best beaches, Silver Beach, and is a centre of the pearl trade. Opened to Western traders in 1876, Beihai has a legacy of colonial architecture. A strong Christian influence is preserved in a 19th-century French cathedral located on the nearby coral island of Weizhou.

Dalian, Liaoning Province

Dalian, also known as Luda, is a thriving port (the third largest in China), summer resort and industrial city of 2 million. Because of a history of foreign occupation, the city is an eclectic medley of architectural styles: China seasoned with a dash of Japan, a pinch of old Russia and a forcible hint of Soviet socialist realism, interspersed with European-style buildings from the 19th and early 20th century. Its Safari Park is home to Siberian tigers. *(See picture, page 195)*

Fuzhou, Fujian Province

On the coast halfway between Shanghai and Guangzhou, Fuzhou is the capital of Fujian Province, and was one of the Treaty Ports open to foreign settlement in the 19th century. The population is a fascinating mix of Minnanhua-speaking locals of Portuguese descent, economic migrants from the poverty-stricken countryside and Shanghainese incomers looking for profit in a rapidlyexpanding city. Fuzhou is still famous for traditional handicrafts, especially the lacquerware with as many as 80 coats of lacquer. Thousand-year-old temples and pagodas stand on nearby hillsides notably on Gushan and Yushan.

Hainan

This tropical island off the southern tip of China is the country's smallest, southernmost and newest province (it was part of Guangdong until it became a Special Economic Zone in 1988). Hainan provides China with coffee, coconuts, sugar and rubber – and is being promoted as an island of tropical resorts. The original inhabitants, members of the Li and Miao minorities, live in the rainforests of the interior, preserving a rich folklore; Han Chinese make up most of the coastal population. The island's biggest city, Haikou (on the north shore), has a bustling street life. The best beaches are in Yalong Bay National Resorts near Sanya in the south – considered the finest stretches of sand in China – and at the newly developed Boao Scenic Zone to the east.

> Fuzhou still contains European-style buildings dating from the 19th century in the 'Three Lanes and Seven Alleys' district, although much of the colonial architecture has given way to skyscrapers.

Huangguoshu Falls, Guizhou Province

China's premier run of cascades and waterfalls, Huangguoshu Falls is as wide as 81m (263ft) and drops a resounding 74m (230ft) in the course of 2km (1 mile). There are also caves to explore, tunnels to walk and a minority

Cosmopolitan Dalian is a popular seaside resort

people, the Bouyei, to meet. Between the great falls and the nearest cities, Anshun and Guiyang, the lush karst landscape of Guizhou Province contains many underground marvels, including Zhingin Cave, China's largest.

Jiayuguan, Gansu Province

Located on the far western edge of old China in the Hexi Corridor, Jiayuguan is the 'mouth' of China and the terminus of the Great Wall. Jiayuguan Fort, built in 1372 under the Ming Dynasty, retains its fortifications and towers. A Great Wall Museum has been added, and there are some 10,000 underground tombs of royal officials nearby, including the 1,700-year-old Wei-Jin tombs now open to visitors.

Jingdezhen, Jiangxi Province

Jingdezhen has been producing famous pottery on the banks of the Yangzi River since the Han dynasty. White clay from a nearby mountain made possible the very thin, durable, translucent porcelain. (The mountain, Gaoling, gave its name to kaolin, the clay used to make porcelain.) Most of the tourist attractions are pottery-oriented: a traditional porcelain producer, a museum, an ancient kiln and modern factories that turn out copies of classic designs.

Lhasa, Tibet

Only tourists in good physical condition should venture to the capital of the Tibet (Xizang) Autonomous Region, for the altitude of 3,600m (nearly 12,000ft) taxes heart and lungs. (Oxygen is provided in the guesthouse and on the sightseeing buses.) In any event, determined travellers find accommodation rather scarce and very expensive. Apart from the majestic Himalayan scenery, the top attraction in Lhasa is the Potala – a fabulous 13-storey building combining the functions of palace, fortress, monastery and dungeon. Other temples, reopened since Beijing granted the Tibetans greater religious freedom in 1980, are now on the itinerary led by Jokhang Temple, Tibet's most active shrine. Increasingly Lhasa is taking on the cast of yet another Chinese city and in 2001 China

Lhasa's loftiest and most famous landmark: the Potala Palace

announced its vision for a modern Tibet, embracing private enterprise and tourism. The city is due to expand by 50 percent over the next 15 years, and the pace of change will accelerate with the completion of the Golmud–Lhasa railway.

The Tibet-Qinghai Railway was completed in 2005. Passengers and freight for the first time in history can travel by train all the way to Beijing from the capital of Tibet. Some 80 percent of the rail route from Lhasa to Golmud is at an elevation of 4,000m (13,000ft). Passenger cars are equipped with tanks of oxygen.

Ningbo, Zhejiang Province

Situated down the coast from Shanghai, this port town has a long history of overseas connections. First it was involved in trade with Japan. Then the Portuguese arrived and settled here. Finally, a British consulate was established in the town after the end of the Opium Wars. The sights include a Ming dynasty library (Tianyi Pavilion) in a pretty garden and a lively pedestrian avenue of old shops and cafes near the Drum Tower. Ningbo is the gateway to one of China's holiest mountains, Putuoshan, the island home of Guanyin, the Buddhist Goddess of Mercy.

Pingyao, Shanxi Province

The small Shanxi walled town of Pingyao, 100km (60 miles) south of Taiyuan, is delightful. A prosperous market town, and later banking centre, during the Ming and Qing dynasties, Pingyao is enclosed within an intact 6km (4 mile) Ming dynasty wall. The town is a wonderful museum of Ming and Qing architecture, old courtyard houses and family residences, and a UNESCO World Heritage site since 1997. Wandering around Pingyao is the best way to absorb its charm; take in such highlights as the Rishengchang bank (dating from 1824), the City Wall, County Yamen and the Town Gods Temple (Chenghuang Miao). North of Pingyao, the Qiao Family Courtyard was the setting for director Zhang Yimou's classic film starring Gong Li, *Raise the Red Lantern*.

➤ Qufu, Shandong Province

The birthplace of Confucius has been turned into an architectural ensemble on the scale of the Forbidden City in Beijing. The memorial temple, Kong Miao, was begun in 478BC, the year after the philosopher's death, and improvements continued for another 2,000 years. The compound itself contains ceremonial gateways, palaces, pavilions, shrines and a thousand carved stone tablets, dominated by the 11th-century Pavilion of the Constellation of Scholars (Kuiwenge) and the 18th-century Hall of Great Achievements (Dacheng Dian), once the venue for sacrificial rites in honour of the sage. The adjacent Confucius Mansions (Kong Fu) consists of hundreds of family halls and rooms. The tombs of Confucius and most of his descendants are set amid ancient pines and cypresses in Confucius Forest (Kong Lin), to the north of the town.

Shanhaiguan, Hebei Province

This walled town's strategic location made it the site of many important battles over thousands of years. This is the site where general Wu Sangui let in the Qing armies, effectively sealing the demise of the Ming dynasty. But it is best known as the eastern terminus of the Great Wall. Five huge Chinese characters meaning 'The First Pass Under Heaven' mark the two-tiered gate-tower as the starting point of the Wall. Today, huge housing developments and highways surround the small town that is confined by ancient city walls and has streets too narrow for public buses. Just south of Shanhaiguan is Laolongtou, where the Great Wall meets the sea.

Shenyang, Liaoning Province

In 1625 Shenyang (better known abroad by its Manchurian name of Mukden) became the Manchu capital. The Imperial Palace (Gugong) they built was intended to rival the Forbidden City of Beijing; some 70 buildings contain 300 rooms. It now serves as a museum of history and archaeology. In the 1930s the 'Mukden Incident' (a bomb explosion on the railway here) precipitated the Japanese occupation of Manchuria. Today more than half of the Manchu ethnic minority live in Shenyang. The city's attractions also include the tomb (Beiling) of the Founder of the Qing Dynasty and the Botanical gardens, interlaced with scores of suspension bridges.

Shenzhen, Guangdong Province

Veteran travellers remember Shenzhen merely as an undistinguished border town on the Hong Kong–Canton railway line. However, it has long been the centre of a Special Economic Zone for joint industrial ventures with capitalists from Hong Kong and Macau. Since 1980, it has become China's richest city, a rival in miniature to Singapore, Seoul, Tokyo and Hong Kong. The streets are straight and clean, the build-

Shenzhen is a prosperous, forward-looking modern city

ings tall and shiny, and the general atmosphere bustling and rich, although rather characterless. With beaches, hot springs and theme parks nearby, the tourist potential has also been rapidly developed. Day tours from Hong Kong offer Shenzhen as a glimpse of life in modern China and a chance to shop at true factory outlets.

Shijiazhuang, Hebei Province

This railway junction has grown into a provincial capital of almost 700,000 people. Shijiazhuang's top sight is the **Hebei Provincial Museum** (Hebei Sheng Bowuguan; open Tues–Sun 8.30– 11.30am and 2–5.30pm). It has a wonderful collection, which includes two Han dynasty jade burial suits designed for Prince Liusheng and his wife Douwan. The ancient temples and pagodas in Zhengding, 18km (11 miles) north of town, make a

Tianjin: a busy trading port, noted for its carpet industry

splendid excursion. The 21-m (69-ft) high bronze statue of Guanyin in Longxing Temple is of particular interest. Worth a day trip, 90km (56 miles) to the southwest is Cangyanshan Mountain, with its spectacular Hanging Palace, and Zhaozhou Bridge, 40kn (25 miles) to the southeast, China's oldest surviving bridge (circa AD 600).

Taiyuan, Shanxi Province

With a history of more than 2,000 years, this provincial capital now makes iron, steel, heavy machinery and fertiliser. Many of the city's historical sights were reduced to rubble during a bloody People's Liberation Army struggle against the Nationalists. The Shanxi Provincial Museum contains revolutionary displays and historic bronzes, ceramics, sculptures and paintings. The Jinci temple complex, 25km (16 miles) southwest of the city, is thought to be more than 1,000 years old, consisting of nearly a hundred pavilions, halls, terraces and bridges. Most impressive is the ancient wooden **Temple of the Holy Mother** (Shengmudian), with life-sized statues reflecting a real humanit. North of Taiyuan is one of Buddhism's Four Famous Peaks, Wutai Shang, with scores of ancient shrines.

Tianjin (Tientsin)

The largest port in northern China, just 120km (74 miles) from Beijing, Tianjin is one of China's most important transport and industrial centres. A large number of historical sights can be found in this municipality of over 9 million people, including an impressive concentration of concession-era Western architecture along Jiefang Beilu. Tianjin's most famous temple is the **Monastery of Deep Compassion** in the north of town (Dabeichan Yuan; open daily 9am–4.30pm). The city has restored two old areas for visitors, a Culture Street (Guwenhuajie) of traditional shops selling books, porcelain, carpets, crafts and food, and a Food Street (Shipinjie) with a hundred outlets offering everything from French fries to Tianjin's native speciality, *goubuli baozi*, steamed buns filled with meat and vegetables.

Weifang, Shandong Province

Weifang is noted for its handicrafts, producing silver mosaic lacquerware, imitations of ancient bronze, kernel carvings, cloth toys, woodcut New Year pictures – and, above all, kites. More kites are produced in Weifang than anywhere else in China, and the international kite festival held here every 20–21 April attracts more than 300,000 visitors, nearly doubling the town's population. Weifang maintains an extensive kite museum, and the local village of Yangjiabu offers kite-making demonstrations at its factory outlet.

A Dai village in tropical Xishuangbanna

Xishuangbanna, Yunnan Province

Tourism is in full throttle in this Autonomous Prefecture (capital: Jinghong) on the border of Burma and Laos. Its population is mostly of the Dai nationality (closely related to the people of Thailand). Large areas of rainforest survive in the humid tropical climate, with thousands of species of trees and plants, and many rare mammals, birds and insects.

Wild elephants, gibbons and the endangered golden monkey are among the protected species. Popular tourist excursions include visits to Dai stilt villages especially during the mid–April Water-splashing Festival and safaris to the Banna Wild Elephant Valley in the Sanchahe Nature Reserve. More adventurous souls can hire a personal guide in Jinghong and explore the jungle and remote villages independently.

Yan'an, Shaanxi Province

This small town in the hills north of Xi'an is one of contemporary China's most celebrated historical sites. In 1937 this was the last stop of the 10,000-km (6,000-mile) odyssey of the Long March. Yan'an's stark landscape of windswept sandstone cliffs provided the backdrop for the 'birthplace of the revolution', and was the headquarters of the Chinese Communist Party for nine years. The city now symbolises the heroic and idealistic phase of the revolution, and many tour groups make the same pilgrimage as Mao Zedong and his followers. Revolutionary landmarks, including the caves in which Mao lived, are the attractions here.

Yantai, Shandong Province

Fishing craft enliven the port of Yantai (known as Chefoo when the British made it a treaty port). The are also a few outdoor markets and a neighbourhood of well-preserved Western-style buildings. The Yantai Museum is architecturally most impressive, and a well spruced-up crop of former colonial consulates – British, Danish, American, Japanese – can be found on the slopes of Yantaishan Park, along with a Ming Dynasty temple. Yantai also has a number of notable beaches, including a popular sandy one down the coast.

> **Northwest of Yantai is Penglai, a magical castle often associated with mythological gods, and famous for the Penglai Mirage. Some witnesses see only a hazy mist while others claim to see entire towns complete with people, buildings and vehicles.**

Yixing, Jiangsu Province

The province's biggest producer of both bamboo and tea, Yixing on Lake Tai is better known for its ceramics. Local pottery production has a history of more than 3,000 years – longer than local recorded history. The industry's heyday was during the Ming dynasty, but recently there has been a revival, encouraged by government support for a National Pottery Centre. 'Purple Sand' teapots in original designs are highly prized and can be purchased at factories in Dingshan village or at roadside markets.

Yixing is Jiangsu Province's main producer of bamboo

Yueyang, Hunan Province

Flamboyant upswept roofs surmount Yueyang Tower, a Tang landmark that has been rebuilt in Song dynasty style. This three-tiered tower overlooks Lake Dongting, the second largest freshwater lake in China. In summer months huge lotus flowers rise above the surface of the water. Junshan, an island in the lake endowed with many hills (and numerous legends), produces the rare and fragrant 'silver needle' tea.

Zhengzhou, Henan Province

This area was first settled more than 3,000 years ago, and traces of the Shang dynasty city wall can still be seen east and northeast of the city centre. Better preserved ancient relics can be viewed in the Henan Provincial Museum. They include some of the earliest forms of Chinese writing: characters inscribed on bones and tortoise shells as well as fossilised dinosaur eggs from the region.

WHAT TO DO

Most visitors to China come to see the nation's many excellent historic and cultural sites, including the imperial treasures. But there is much else of interest in this vast land to make the journey truly enjoyable. You will, of course, want to bring home at least a few souvenirs, and you will have opportunities to attend presentations of an incredible range of performing arts. It will not be difficult to fill your moments of leisure with memorable activities that will make your trip last well after you return home.

SHOPPING

With incomes shooting up across the nation, China's shopping culture has undergone a revolution since the early 1990s. Most large towns now have huge department stores, and vast hypermarkets, such as the French chain Carrefour, can be found in Beijing, Shanghai, Tianjin and beyond. Many of the big cities have multistorey shopping centres with

> Prices are fixed by the government at department stores, so it is useful to check prices there before buying a similar item on the free market.

brand names and fancy cafes. Electronics can be bought from big name domestic stores like GOME while a range of cheaper electrical goods are sold in big supermarkets. Silks, teas, jade and porcelain are sold in shops and markets in tourist areas. Many of the bigger department stores take credit cards but it is advisable to bring cash just in case. Shopping malls generally have a cluster of ATMs on the ground floor which usually allow withdrawals on overseas debit and credit cards. Shopping around should certainly give you the chance of finding similar items at better

Magnificent Chinese lanterns make wonderful, though fragile, souvenirs

prices. (Avoid buying artworks and souvenirs from hotel shops, where prices there tend to be very expensive). The big department stores are no longer state-owned institutions, and new stores and malls are opening all the time. Symbols of the consumer revolution include the vast Oriental Plaza on Dongchang'an Jie in Beijing and the enormous Nextage in Shanghai's Pudong district.

In many cities, arts and crafts department stores showcase the output of local artisans. Antiques shops specialise in old pottery, jewellery, carvings and calligraphy, as well as high-quality reproductions. Since the distribution system is unpredictable, old China hands say you shouldn't take a chance: if you find something you like, buy it, for it might not be on sale anywhere else.

Fruit, vegetables, fish and meat are sold at markets. In the free markets, where prices are more flexible, and sometimes higher (reflecting better quality goods and greater availability), there are often other items such as wicker baskets, metalwork and clothes. In the bigger cities, street traders offer their wares well into the evening.

> **Bargaining is often essential, although it is inadvisable in state-owned shops or department stores. At markets, however, it is imperative, especially as foreigners tend to be overcharged. Be polite but firm when haggling and don't be afraid to walk away if the price is unacceptable.**

What to Buy

Bargains are rare, but there's much to buy in China's department stores, shops and markets. Here's an alphabetical listing to start you on your rounds.

Antiques. From fossils to ancient coins, Chinese customs regulations prohibit the export of any cultural relics dating from before 1795. Even more recent antiques may not be legally exported unless they are marked with a special red wax seal. All other antiques are the property of the People's Republic of China and, without the seal, will be confiscated without compensation if you try to take them out of the country. Even

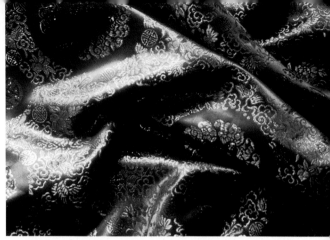

Chinese silk has been eagerly bought by foreigners for centuries

so, browsing is fascinating. Remember that many knowledge-able buyers will have preceded you. Remember, too, that pro-ducing fake 'antiques' (accompanied by fake official seals) is a thriving industry and that much of what you see is likely to be counterfeit.

Bamboo products. In the southern regions where bamboo grows, cottage industries turn out bamboo tea boxes, fans, flutes, chopsticks, walking sticks and furniture.

Brocades and silk. Since the Han Dynasty, China has been exporting delicate silk fabrics in brilliant colours. These days you can buy inexpensive raw silk by the metre or exquisite brocades, as well as beautifully made silk scarves, ties, shirts and blouses.

Bronzeware. Modern versions of traditional hotpots are use-ful in the home, as are bronze pitchers, plates and vases (often engraved with intricate dragon or floral designs).

Carpets and rugs. Luxurious and colourful, Oriental rugs of wool or silk are a tempting buy. The big stores catering to for-eign tourists can arrange for shipping.

China (porcelain). Reproductions of classical designs or modern teapots, cups, plates, bowls, spoons and vases. Shrewd buyers point out that price tags always indicate the excellence of porcelain (and of cloisonné ware, too). In the line of Chinese text before the actual price, look for the Chinese symbols for the numerals 1, 2 or 3 (one, two or three horizontal lines), meaning first, second or third class. If there's no number at all, it means first class.

Chopsticks. You might want to collect the appropriate utensils. Elaborate chopsticks are sold in their own fitted carrying cases – handy for a picnic or an emergency.

Cloisonné. The Chinese don't claim to have invented this type of enamelware decoration, but they have been doing it very well for several hundred years. Cloisonné is applied to plates, vases and other items.

Ethnic novelties. Artisans from China's ethnic minority groups produce a good share of exotica: ornaments and figurines,

Chinese warriors at Beijing's Panjiayuan Market

ceremonial knives and swords, skullcaps and other headgear, colourful dresses and shirts, and shaggy sheepskin coats.

Fans. One factory in Hangzhou alone manufactures 10 million fans per year, most of them for export. They come in several hundred varieties, but the best known folding fans are made of fragrant sandalwood or black paper.

Figurines. Ceramic polychrome figurines of historic or legendary personages are very popular, as are little animals, especially the giant panda.

Furniture. Screens, chairs and chests made of boxwood, mahogany or bamboo and decorated with elaborately carved designs re-create the atmosphere of old China. Shipping abroad can be arranged.

Furs. Sable or marten coats are often displayed in Friendship Stores. The styling might not be the latest fashion, but the cheap price tag could make all the difference.

You should not export – or even buy in the first place – objects made from wild animals, especially from ivory. Ivory carvings of remarkable intricacy are a Chinese speciality, but today substitute materials are used to good effect. You are unlikely to find anything made from genuine tusk. If you did – and could afford it – it would surely be confiscated when you arrived home.

Ginseng. The all-purpose Chinese medicinal herb is becoming well known and popular in the West as a tonic. Small doses of ginseng in tea, wine or soup are claimed to be the secret of enduring vitality.

Herbs and spices. Every market has stands selling fragrant spices. Look above all for varieties that are particular to the region; in Chongqing, for instance, you might buy Sichuan dried peppers. A few *fen* will buy an exotic gift, which will be especially welcome when the herbs or spices are unknown or unavailable at home.

Jade. One of the hardest of stones, jade has intrigued the Chinese for at least 3,000 years, and has been used to make everything from Han dynasty funeral robes to Qing dynasty vases. It is a symbol of nobility and is worn for several reasons: as good luck, as a protection against sickness and as an amulet for travellers. Even if you don't believe in its mystical powers, jade's aesthetic appeal cannot be denied. Do not buy from open-air private markets unless you are confident that you know real jade from imitation.

Kites. In windy Beijing and many other Chinese cities, high-flying kites are a favourite of both children and adults. The designs are colourful, original and elaborate.

Lacquerware. Numerous layers of lacquer, individually polished, are applied to trays, cups, vases and boxes. Lacquer also makes the ideal finish for tea and coffee services, since the material resists boiling water as well as the tannins and other chemicals in tea and coffee.

Luggage. One answer to the problem of excessive buying might be to buy additional luggage to carry your souvenirs home. The Chinese make good, cheap, sturdy suitcases of all sizes. Or you can pick up a local imitation of a Western executive attaché case.

Traditional themes are reproduced by modern painters

Musical instruments. Such European and Chinese musical instruments as the violin, guitar, flute and pipa (a plucked stringed instrument) are well made and usually well priced in China.

Paintings. Squadrons of Chinese artists copy traditional drawings and paintings by hand. A lengthy scroll can take as long as ten days to complete, brushstroke by brushstroke, with the details of a landscape intended to be viewed in sections, not all at once. Artists also produce original meditations on venerable themes. The scrolls have the distinct advantage of being ready rolled, which makes them easy to pack.

Paper art. The Chinese, who invented paper, are thought to have devised the decorative art of paper cutting nearly 2,000 years ago. With great skill, scissors-wielding paper cutters produce intricate scenes suitable for framing.

Rubbings and reproductions. Stone rubbings of inscriptions from ancient temples, or of classical calligraphy on stone pillars, make popular (and portable) souvenirs. In some museums you

Open-air markets are often the source of bargains

will find shops selling reproductions of their most famous archaeological exhibits (for example, the flying horse of Wuwei in Lanzhou). Tiny facsimiles of the Xi'an warriors are now available all over China.

Seals. These ink stamps (also called 'chops') are the traditional Chinese substitute for handwritten signatures. You can have one carved specifically for you, with your name incised – perhaps in ancient Chinese block characters – in soapstone, plastic or jade.

Souvenirs. In any local department store or street market you're likely to come across some very Chinese inspirations: acupuncture charts and dolls, those ubiquitous thermos flasks, tea mugs with lids, padded jackets, posters and so on.

Tea. A collection of Chinese teas (black, green, semi-fermented and flower-petal) makes an inexpensive and useful

Masks make good souvenirs

souvenir. Tea is often pack-aged in special, artistically decorated containers.

Toys. Cheap and unusual toys, from cuddly animals to mechanical games, are being manufactured in increasing numbers in China.

Woollens. An unexpected bargain is cashmere sweaters, in all styles and colours. Other woollens, too, can be economical, good-quality purchases.

ENTERTAINMENT

After a gruelling day of sightseeing, you might not be too disap-pointed to discover that, in most of China, an evening's enter-tainment starts and ends early. Except in Shanghai, Guangzhou and Beijing, most restaurants close well before midnight, and theatres and concerts generally finish before 10pm.

Chinese Opera

The Chinese hospitably assume that foreigners can't bear more than about 10 minutes of traditional Chinese opera. You might, indeed, find the voices shrill and the mannerisms maddening (many characters seem to spend most of the time fussing with their sleeves, which can unroll to the floor). So you should not mind if your guide or host rushes you out of the theatre into the early evening traffic.

But if you persevere, you will begin to understand what the Chinese see in this age-old art form. If you fail, you've still enjoyed the splendid costumes and make-up, the acrobatics that enliven some regional versions, and the experience of sharing a theatrical occasion with local people. Chinese opera combines amusement with edification in a glittering package few Western impresarios could afford to mount. Peking opera is the version that is most familiar to Westerners, but other regions have their own variants.

If possible, familiarise yourself with the plot in advance. Ideologically uplifting operas were the only ones permitted during the Cultural Revolution; classical stories were banned. But today both classical and modern works are presented. If you have an interpreter at hand, you'll understand why some scenes animate the audience and others don't. The words of the songs are projected onto screens alongside the proscenium to clarify the nuances of a tonal language set to music.

Apart from the set pieces, most of the music is percussive and serves to support and reflect the action and mood. Props are minimal and the action is subtle: an actor closes an invisible door with a mime gesture, anyone walking with a riding crop must be understood to be mounted on a horse, and carrying an oar shows that the action takes place on a boat.

The characters in Peking opera are identified by stylised costumes

The costumes are similarly stylised and symbolic, and based on court costumes of the Han, Tang, Song and especially Ming dynasties. Make-up is equally important: the make-up artists can create more than 300 different types of mask-like faces. Audiences need not go to the same sartorial lengths: normal day clothes are quite acceptable at the opera.

Puppets, Acrobats and Folklore Groups

Popular with adults and children, Chinese shadow play (a 2,000-year-old art form) dramatises familiar legends. The two-dimensional puppets, manipulated by puppeteers behind a silk screen, can jump and fly, giving the colourful silhouettes an advantage over the actors in Chinese opera. The busy puppeteers give voice to their characters, often in song. Professional and amateur shadow-play troupes also put on shows with marionettes.

The so-called acrobatic shows are more fun than you might expect. The trapeze artists, of course, are first-class, and so are the contortionists and human pyramid acts. But they also include jugglers, magicians, animal acts and even clowns, and you don't have to understand a word to join in the laughter. Almost every large town has its troupe of acrobats, many of

The Greatest Name in Opera

Mei Lanfang (1894–1961) remains without question China's most celebrated opera singer. Famous from the age of the 20, he sang more than a thousand *dan* (heroine) roles during his long career (this key female character in Peking opera is traditionally played by a man). Not only a performer but also a choreographer, he became the foreign ambassador for this ancient Chinese art: he appeared in Japan, in Russia and in the United States, where he toured in 1929 – and forged a friendship with Charlie Chaplin. Berthold Brecht attended the performance that Mei gave in Moscow in 1935. Today, his son Mei Baojiu continues the family tradition.

which tour the country. In big cities such as Beijing, Shanghai and Guangzhou, there are permanent performances.

Typically, the 'Chinese folklore' performances are organised especially for tourists. Shows feature the costumes, songs and dances of the national minority groups – often as foreign to a Chinese audience as they are to visitors from abroad. These evenings are usually uplifting and not very long.

Concerts and Ballet

During the Cultural Revolution, Beethoven and Tchaikovsky were banned and many musicians banished to the countryside for 're-education'.

Traditional acrobatic shows are staged throughout China

So if you go to a concert today, you'll sense the drama of recovery from mad xenophobia. This needn't obscure the fact that some professional musicians haven't yet reached world standards. But the enthusiasm of players and audience is exciting in itself.

Ballet, which was a vehicle for ideological indoctrination during the 1960s and 1970s, is much less restricted today. Folk legends are often a source of inspiration, and classical European works are sometimes performed, with elaborate costumes, sets and lighting effects.

Nightlife

In Beijing, Shanghai and Guangzhou you will find a selection of English-language free magazines aimed at expatriates featuring local nightlife and entertainment listings. The That's series – *That's Beijing*, *That's Shanghai* and *That's Guangzhou* – are recommended, and Beijing now has its own *Time Out* magazine. These publications list restaurants, cafes, bars, clubs and art galleries. The magazines can usually be picked up from western-style bars and restaurants and some of the bigger hotels.

In the larger cities, many bars and clubs have opened in recent years, and are now meeting places for affluent youths. Far more common, however, are karaoke bars. The Japanese-style sing-along bars have swept China, increasing the planet's off-key harmonies considerably. Most are easily recognised by the letters 'OK' among the characters for their names. Some of these bars are pricey, with the clientele being rich businessmen; some are fronts for prostitution.

The Festival of Lanterns marks the end of the New Year holiday

Clubs are popular throughout China and can be found in a number of towns. Many hotels have their own discos, which are frequented by well-off local youths. Many discos, particularly in the hotels, stay open till the early hours of the morning.

With varying degrees of success, the tourist hotels try to meet foreigners' demands for a quiet place to have an evening drink and a chat. Only the newest hotels, those built with international co-operation, contain bars reminiscent of those found in Europe or America. The others are likely to be quaint rather than cosy.

Traditional Festivals

All official Chinese holidays are of modern invention, commemorating the triumphs of the international working class or the Chinese Communist Party *(see Holidays, page 240)*. The festivals listed below, however, are traditional rather than 'official', and provide excellent opportunities for visitors to experience Chinese culture at its best.

Chinese New Year or Spring Festival. The year's most important festival, the Lunar New Year, is also called the Spring Festival in China. On the Gregorian calendar it can come at any time during the month that begins about 21 January, which is somewhat early for spring-like weather. The country's only three-day holiday, it is a family occasion, a time for buying new clothes, giving and receiving gifts, paying debts and eating well. The holiday ends with the Lantern Festival, a carnival of light and noise.

Qingming. This April festival is a time for honouring ancestors. The sweeping of graves, a traditional obligation, is not as solemn as it sounds.

Dragon Boat Festival. On the fifth day of the fifth lunar month – usually in July – this celebration recalls the ancient poet and statesman Qu Yuan (340–278BC), who drowned in Hunan Province in spite of all efforts to save him. The population threw rice cakes into the river, to try to stop the fish devouring his body. Today sweet rice cakes made with dates or nuts are served. Some cities organise dragon-boat races, sometimes involving crews from around the world.

Mid-Autumn Festival. The date depends on when the harvest moon reaches its fullest – usually around mid-September. Everyone turns out to toast the full moon and hope for a big harvest. The shops do great business in 'moon cakes' (pastries filled with gooey sesame paste, red-bean and walnut filling) and *tang yuan* (glutinous rice-flour balls with sweet fillings in sugar syrup).

Confucius Festival. Late September is normally the time when Chinese communities celebrate the memory of Confucius.

Christmas. November and December are relatively quiet months in China but Christmas is gaining momentum as a consumer celebration. Christian churches hold special services that draw thousands of spectators. In Beijing, it is fashionable to exchange Christmas cards and presents, and there are even sightings of Santa Claus in some shops.

EATING OUT

While Europeans were still dining on porridge and gnawing bones, the art of good cooking was becoming an important part of China's cultural heritage. French *haute cuisine* competes with it for subtlety and sophistication, although the Chinese have been gourmets a couple of thousand years longer. To this day, no other people prepare such a vast variety of dishes from so wide a choice of ingredients, presented with such sensitivity and flair.

Almost every country in the world now has Chinese restaurants. But the authenticity of the food suffers greatly when essential ingredients are hard to come by and the chef compromises with local tastes. Real Chinese cuisine can be one of the highlights of your trip, as memorable as Peking opera or a walk on the Great Wall *(see page 247 for more advice)*.

WHAT TO EAT

Hunger, a familiar plague in the nation's history, inspired the Chinese people to make the most of foods others might have

Cantonese starters: spring rolls and steamed dumplings

deemed inedible – snakes, certain fish, and the lining gathered from swifts' nests. Large animals that require pasture lands – cows and sheep, for example – are not as common as poultry and the ubiquitous pig. Without doubt, pork is the most popular meat. In addition, both fresh and saltwater fish are highly prized and usually well prepared.

Vegetables are of supreme importance, but are rarely eaten raw. This stems partly from hygienic considerations, as the traditional fertiliser was human waste. The range of vegetables cultivated in China is vast, particularly in the warmer south, and includes exotic delights such as a huge range of leafy greens, bamboo shoots, water chestnuts, taro and lotus root.

The most common method of cooking is stir-frying in a wok over a very high heat. Not only does this save fuel, but it results in both crisp texture and maximum vitamin retention. Deep-frying, steaming and braising are also popular, but slowly roasted or baked meats are not, and are usually produced only in restaurant kitchens.

Shanghai restaurants proclaim their wares with gaudy signs

Few Chinese dishes feature any one ingredient exclusively. The harmonious blending of ingredients and balance of seasoning is important; common seasonings are soy sauce, ginger, garlic, vinegar, sesame oil, soybean paste and spring onions. The Chinese revel in culinary contrasts: bitter and sweet, crunchy and tender, the yellow of the pineapple and the red of the pepper.

In choosing Chinese food, individual tastes tend to be subordinated to the general welfare. All the dishes are shared; thus, the more people there are in your party the more opportunities you will have to sample many flavours. Using chopsticks lengthens the reach, so serving dishes don't have to be passed around, although large circular tables sometimes have revolving platters to facilitate the distribution of the food.

Surviving a Banquet

Tourist groups are often offered banquets or formal dinners, in which protocol problems compound any uncertainty over the food. The Chinese are most understanding about foreigners' gaffes, but here are a few guidelines to help you avoid making a *faux pas*.

Don't be late. Don't touch any of the food or drink until your host gives the sign that the proceedings have begun. Drink the firewater (usually *mao tai*) in your smallest glass *only* when toasting or replying to a toast. Taste a bit of every dish offered, but start sparingly, for there might be as many as 13 courses. One by one, the prepared dishes are placed in the centre of the table. You should help yourself with a serving spoon, if provided, or with your own chopsticks. Don't take the last morsel from a serving dish; this might imply that not enough food has been provided. Don't ask for rice, which is not served at banquets; it would be tantamount to demanding a sandwich at a formal dinner.

Regional Cuisines

Profound regional variations developed in Chinese cooking as some ingredients were readily available in one area and not another: tastes, like the climate, differ from place to place.

Most Chinese restaurants overseas feature Cantonese food because it was people from the southern Guangdong Province (formerly 'Canton') who emigrated far and wide, opened restaurants and introduced new tastes. Cantonese chefs are renowned for their creativity and willingness to incorporate foreign ingredients. They make abundant use of fruit and many types of vegetables, as well as seafood such as prawn, abalone, squid

> With a little practice, anyone can use chopsticks. Wedge one stick in the V between your thumb and index finger, resting it on your ring finger. Hold the other between the tips of your thumb, index and middle fingers. This is the one you pivot to grasp food.

Fresh fruit for sale at a Beijing market

and crab. Steaming and stir-frying methods capture the natural flavour – as well as the colour and vitamins – of Cantonese food. Look for steamed dumplings filled with meat or shrimp, deep-fried spring rolls and, of course, sweet-and-sour pork or prawns. Steamed white rice is the usual accompaniment, although you can order fried rice instead.

Wheat, not rice, is the staple in the north of China, where meals involve noodles or steamed bread or dumplings. Most northern cuisine stems from Shandong Province, but with some influences from Mongolian and Hebei cooking. Beijing is the place to try Mandarin Fish, Thousand-Layer Cake and the legendary delicacy Peking Duck. Every day, restaurants in the capital turn out thousands of freshly roasted, crispy-skinned ducks. Diners wrap small pieces of skin and meat, sprinkled with green onions and anointed with a sweet bean sauce, in the thinnest of pancakes.

Time and great care go into the cooking and preparation of Shanghai cuisine. The flavours are full of happy surprises: sweet or salt accents, plus hints of garlic or vinegar. Meats are often marinated, then braised at length in soy sauce, wine and sugar.

However, Shanghai is best known for its seafood, with such dishes as steamed freshwater crab, honey-fried eel, braised yellowfish and sautéed shrimp (prawns). Nearby Hangzhou has a subtle novelty, shrimp in tea sauce, permeated with the unobtrusive flavour of locally grown tea.

Sichuan Province is the source of the peppery Szechuan recipes, which are much more complicated than the first fiery taste would indicate. They combine many elements in unlikely coexistence: bitter, sweet, fruity, tart and sour. Even beancurd, which many tourists consider hopelessly bland, takes on real character in the hands of cooks in Chengdu or Chongqing. But not everything on the Sichuan menu is hot; for a bit of relief, try sautéed shredded pork with spring onions and soybeans.

Neighbouring Hunan Province also revels in the invigorating possibilities of the chilli pepper. But dishes here turn out less spicy and oily than in their Sichuan counterparts. The gourmets rave about Hunan's chilli-smoked pork or chicken.

Wherever you travel in China, look for the local specialities: roast lamb and pilaf rice in far-west Xinjiang, great hunks of

The Fast Food Invasion

American-style fast food has become so popular in Chinese cities that parents are concerned about the effects it is having on their children's health. Despite campaigns to encourage the creation of fast-food restaurants serving Chinese specialities, the American brand names are rampant.

Kentucky Fried Chicken now has more than 1,000 stores in China. KFC was the first fast-food chain to invade China, opening a restaurant close to Tiananmen Square in 1987. McDonald's arrived later, in 1992, but has now established itself all over the country. According to recent studies, Chinese students eat Western-style fast food on average 10 times a month – despite the fact that a hamburger, a portion of fries and a soft drink cost 10 times more than a traditional snack bought from a roadside stall.

mutton in Inner Mongolia, Yunnan's delicately smoked ham served in the thinnest slices, and sweet-and-sour fish along the Yangzi.

In the northeast, Jilin Province is famous for stewed chicken with ginseng. Neighbouring Heilongjiang Province offers such unusual delicacies as stewed moose nose and braised bear paw with pine nuts. The cooks of Guilin proudly prepare steamed bamboo rat, masked civet and – a great winter tonic – snake broth. If you see 'ground goat' on the menu, be aware that this is a euphemism for dog meat, a long-time favourite of Chinese gourmets.

Sanlitun Lu in Beijing is lined with cafés, bars and restaurants

Conventions of the Table

In nearly every hotel in China, Western tourists are automatically served a European/American-style breakfast consisting of eggs, toast, butter, jam and an interpretation of coffee. If you want to try an authentic Chinese breakfast (which typically consists of rice porridge, buns and perhaps noodles and cold appetisers), you will have to convince the waiter that you really mean it.

In provincial or non-tourist restaurants – and occasionally in the better hotels – you'll notice the Chinese habit of wiping chopsticks and bowls with a paper napkin before a meal. No one takes offence at this precaution. In many parts of the country, it is common, and not considered rude, to eat rice by bringing the bowl to the lips and shovelling it in with chopsticks.

Tea is sold in a wide range of flavours and fragrances

WHAT TO DRINK

The Chinese have been enjoying wine for thousands of years. Each province or region has its own wine or liqueur, usually rather sweet. It's made from local fruits, flowers or herbs.

Connoisseurs mention red and white wines from Shanghai and the dry white wine of Yantai. Rice wines come in many varieties; the most venerable is distilled at Shaoxing in Zhejiang Province. In Xi'an you will be offered Xifeng wine, a breathtaking, colourless drink that was first made during the time of the Tang dynasty.

Like the wines, Chinese spirits display regional variations, incorporating ingredients as ingenious as bamboo leaves, chrysanthemums and cloves. The best-known spirit, and the staple for banquet toasts, is *mao tai*, which is fragrant and mellow but quite potent.

Beer drinkers use their frothy superlatives in recommending Tsingtao, the hearty, German-style beer brewed from the spring water of Laoshan Mountain. A number of local brands are also available in various regions, but none has a comparable international reputation. Mineral waters are also available, as are fruit juices and soft drinks based on fruit flavours.

Tea is usually served to guests in an anteroom before a banquet. Teahouses, today something of a rarity in China, are rich in local colour, with musicians or storytellers on hand to entertain customers, who play cards or dominoes by the hour. The Chinese drink their tea without sugar or milk. Among the varieties available are black (fermented) tea, fragrant green tea, tea scented with jasmine or magnolia, and slightly fermented oolong tea.

HANDY TRAVEL TIPS

An A–Z Summary of Practical Information

A

ACCOMMODATION

Accommodation for visitors on package tours is arranged in advance, often in conjunction with the China International Travel Service (CITS). Overseas travel agents can now book rooms with many international-class hotels throughout China's main cities. Individual travellers can make their own advanced bookings through a growing number of international hotel chains: Holiday Inn and Shangri-La have the largest range of hotels in China. Hotels are busiest – and sometimes completely full – in the peak seasons of May, September and October. But if you have confirmed reservations, your room will be waiting for you, as hotels rarely overbook.

Chinese hotels range from first-class to grimly spartan. The newest hotels, often built with foreign cooperation and with foreign management, bear a close resemblance to their counterparts in Europe or America, although service standards frequently fall short. Usually the prices of these better hotels are in line with hotel prices in the West.

More adventurous travellers might prefer the charm of old-fashioned establishments or Chinese-managed hotels and inns in interesting or scenic locations. In general, hotels in small or remote towns offer few comforts.

Worth mentioning are a few well-preserved hotels built by the colonial powers in some cities. They include the Peace Hotel (Heping) in Shanghai, the People's Hotel (Renmin Dasha) in Xi'an and the Astor Hotel (Lishunde Dafandian) in Tianjin. The interiors, of course, have been modernised.

Air-conditioning is ubiquitous, except in the very cheapest of rooms. Telephones are usually provided, and deluxe hotel rooms are equipped with small refrigerators, satellite TV, broadband Internet connection and a wide range of amenities. In almost every room you'll find cups and a large thermos of hot water for making tea; a small container of tea is often supplied as well. Bottled water or water coolers are provided in most quality hotels. As a rule, never drink water from the tap, though some of the top hotels may provide potable tap water.

In the larger Chinese-managed hotels, there is a service desk on each floor with a staff-member who often speaks a bit of English, keeps room keys, handles the laundry, deals with telephone problems and sells cigarettes, snacks, drinks and postcards. Postal and tour desks, a foreign-exchange facility and gift shops are usually located on the ground floor.

A suggestion: when you wander out on your own, even for a brief stroll, take with you a hotel card (usually available from reception or a porter) with the hotel's name printed in Chinese and English – useful when you have to ask the way or give directions to a taxi driver.

AIRPORTS

All internal flights are handled by China's domestic air carriers, which now fly advanced Western-purchased aircraft to most major destinations. At Beijing's Capital Airport, the most popular arrival point for foreign tourists, there are restaurants, snack bars, souvenir stands, a duty-free shop and a post office. There's even a Starbucks. Banks inside the arrivals hall can change foreign currency, and local currency can be withdrawn on several ATMs.

Airport transport. The municipality of Beijing runs airport buses to the city centre. Taxis are also available for the 40-minute journey into town. Many international hotels provide some form of airport shuttle or transfer. Make arrangements with hotels well ahead of your arrival. Near the main entrance there are desks where transfer to city hotels can be arranged. If you are taking a taxi, avoid the hustlers and join the queue of people waiting for a cab on the pavement just outside the terminal. Drivers and touts mill about outside the customs area, but they should be avoided, as they charge twice or three times the going rate for the ride.

CAAC buses also link airports with their offices in numerous towns and cities throughout China. Shanghai's Pudong International Airport is linked to the metro system by a high-speed MagLev train

(430km/h/ 267mph). Several airports in China are situated far from the city centre, so it is important to calculate how long it will take you to reach the airport by taxi or bus.

Arrival. Passengers arriving from abroad hand over health certificates (distributed on the plane) to a health officer, and passports, visas and landing cards to immigration officers, who stamp and return the documents. You will also be given a departure form which you must complete before you depart. Customs procedures are generally straightforward and foreigners are usually paid little attention.

Departure. Be sure to reconfirm your reservation at least 72 hours ahead of your departure (many hotels will do this for you) and arrive at the airport 2 hours before check-in time. Note that you'll be required to pay an airport departure tax, always in Chinese currency. Departure tax is now usually included in the price of the ticket.

B

BICYCLE HIRE

You can hire bicycles in many Chinese towns, either at the hotels or at bike shops. You will have to leave a deposit as security. It is advisable to park your cycle at a guarded parking space for a small fee. China has bicycle thieves and there is a fine for illegal parking.

BUDGETING FOR YOUR TRIP

Prices for tourist accommodation, meals, sightseeing and entertainment bear no relationship to the local cost of living. Goods and services priced on the Chinese scale represent considerable bargains for visitors. To give you a rough idea of what to expect, here are some approximate figures; note that they are subject to regional, seasonal and inflationary variations.

Airport transfer. Taxi from Beijing airport to city about 85 *yuan*.
Car and driver. 400 *yuan* per day (8 hours or 120km/75 miles).
Entertainment. Theatre or Chinese opera 50–200 *yuan*.

Hairdresser. Woman's haircut 70–90 *yuan*; man's haircut 70 *yuan*.

Hotels (double room with bath). Luxury international class 1,200–2,500 *yuan*; moderate 600–1,200 *yuan*. Rates vary according to the season and the location.

Meals and drinks. Lunch in moderate restaurant 30–60 *yuan*; in expensive restaurant 80–150 *yuan*. Dinner in moderate restaurant 80–120 *yuan*; in expensive restaurant 120–320 *yuan*. Imported spirits 50 *yuan* per drink; Chinese beer in bar 15–30 *yuan*; in shop approx. 3 *yuan*; imported beer 40–60 *yuan*. Cup of coffee 10–20 *yuan*.

Museum entry. 2–40 *yuan*.

Transport. City bus 0.5–1 *yuan*. Taxi from Beijing railway station to Tiananmen Square 10 *yuan*; taxi from Beijing Hotel to Temple of Heaven 25 *yuan*.

C

CAR HIRE

Hire cars have been introduced in China, but the industry is in its infancy and there are restrictions on where you can drive. China is not an easy country to drive in for visitors and, although road rules generally match those found in the West, driving conditions are appalling and highly dangerous. Taxis and chauffeur-driven cars are the usual choice, both readily available through hotels. If you don't want to hire a car for the whole day, it's often possible to arrange for a taxi by the hour. Taxis are fairly inexpensive for getting around town (usually 15–50 *yuan* per trip, depending on the distance travelled). Receipts can be provided; insist that the taxi meter is used.

CLIMATE

China is a vast country encompassing a variety of different climates. Summer lasts more than six months of the year in Guangzhou (Canton) but flits past in only 15 days in far western Urumqi. In January the mean temperature in Harbin, in the northeast, is -19°C (-2°F) while

Guangzhou, in the south, basks at 14°C (57°F). In general, the best seasons all over China are spring and autumn, when most areas have moderate temperatures. Some average monthly temperatures:

		J	F	M	A	M	J	J	A	S	O	N	D
Beijing	°F	25	28	39	55	68	77	79	77	68	55	39	27
	°C	-4	-2	4	13	20	25	26	25	20	13	4	-3
Guangzhou	°F	57	59	64	72	79	81	84	84	81	75	68	59
	°C	14	15	18	22	26	27	29	29	27	24	20	15
Shanghai	°F	37	39	46	57	66	75	82	82	75	64	55	43
	°C	3	4	8	14	19	24	28	28	24	18	13	6
Xi'an	°F	27	36	46	57	68	79	81	79	68	55	45	34
	°C	-3	2	8	14	20	26	27	26	20	13	7	1
Guilin	°F	46	48	56	65	74	79	83	82	78	69	59	50
	°C	8	9	13	18	24	26	29	28	26	21	15	10

CLOTHING

Be sure to pack sweaters and rainwear. For winter, a warm overcoat is essential and thermal underwear is a boon; gloves, scarves and hats make worthy accessories. All can be bought on the spot, if necessary, at reasonable prices. The Chinese tend to dress in several layers of clothing, facilitating quick reactions to changes of temperature.

Tourists dress with relative informality, although business visitors should wear suits and ties for important meetings or banquets. In general, try to avoid dressing shabbily. Perhaps the most essential item is a durable pair of walking shoes.

COMMUNICATIONS

Post Offices

Hotels often have branch post offices or postal service desks (open seven days a week), some selling stamps, writing paper and postcards. Chinese envelopes are generally made without glue, and so are some stamps, which explains the presence of a gluepot on the counter. Airmail letters and postcards take up to ten days to reach overseas destinations; surface mail travels very slowly.

The Chinese post office has no facilities for poste restante (general delivery) mail. If you expect to receive mail while in China, ask correspondents to address letters to the hotels where you'll be staying. Courier services are also available in major cities.

Telephone

The country code for China is 86. To dial China directly from abroad, you must first dial the international access code, then 86, then the city code of your destination in China (for example, Beijing's code is 10; Shanghai's is 21), then the local Chinese number.

To make a long-distance call within China (for example, from Beijing to Shanghai), dial 0 plus the city code, then the local number. Domestic long-distance calls are cheap, but international calls are expensive. To make an international direct-dial call from China, dial 00 plus the country code, then the area code and the number. Long-distance phone companies have local access codes that can be used in various Chinese cities to call the US – AT&T: 108 11; MCI: 108 12; Sprint 108 13. Dial 115 for international directory enquiries in English.

Local calls from your hotel may be free (check this before phoning) and are typically very cheap from public phones and kiosks. Coin-operated public phones are rare and most now take IC cards, which can be purchased from streetside kiosks and China Telecom offices. Most hotels provide international direct dialling, usually from your room. The cheapest way to phone abroad is to buy an IP card (widely available); you phone a local number, enter your card number followed by a password number and then dial the number you wish to call. Be aware that telephone numbers in China regularly change without notice. If you have a GSM mobile phone you will be able to use it in China. You may either use your home service on roaming or buy a pre-paid SIM card. They, and top-up cards, are available from airports, telecom stores and roadside kiosks.

Fax and E-mail

A fax service is available in most hotels, often in their business centres. E-mail and Internet services are reasonably widespread in China, although the number of Internet cafés *(wangba)* is smaller than it was a few years ago, after the authorities cracked down on unlicensed operations. Internet cafés usually charge around two *yuan* per hour. Many three to five-star hotels now offer broadband Internet access, so it's worth asking about this. Avoid using hotel business centres to send e-mails, as they are usually very expensive. Many coffee shops, bars and cafes now offer free wireless Internet in the bigger cities such as Beijing and Shanghai.

COMPLAINTS

China's tourist industry is developing at an uneven pace. Formal procedures for complaints have yet to be instituted, although there is a hotline service to answer tourists' complaints in some major cities *(see below)*. The issue is complicated by the matter of 'saving face': public criticism of any individual is deemed unjustifiably cruel. A quiet word with your guide will be far more effective than an open demonstration of dissatisfaction. Losing your temper should be the last resort, but don't be afraid of being firm.

Hotline numbers are as follows:

Beijing	6513-0828	**Shanghai**	6252-0000
Guangzhou	8666-1275	**Tianjin**	835-8814
Hangzhou	8515-6631	**Nanjing**	8342-1125
Kunming	313-5412	**Suzhou**	6522-3377
Jinan	296-3423	**Guilin**	382-7391
Qingdao	582-6555	**Xi'an**	8745-5043

CRIME AND SAFETY

Crime exists in China, as it does in all countries, but official statistics show the incidence is low in comparison with Western societies. Cases of crime against foreign visitors are rare, although it is always wise to be wary of pickpockets and petty thieves around tourist sites, on public buses and in markets. Use a money belt. Avoid accompanying strangers who strike up conversations and offer to act as your guide; not all of them have honourable motives, particularly those of China's destitute 'floating population', which numbers many millions.

Chinese men are generally not intimidating towards women and female travellers usually feel safe travelling in China. You can usually walk freely at any time of day or night without fear, especially in a group. The most common hassles are fending off hustlers eager to sell you something, and avoiding beggars, who can be persistent.

Call the police!	**jiao jing cha**	快叫警察!
Help!	**jiu ren a**	来人哪!
Call a doctor!	**kuai jiao yisheng**	快找医生!
Danger!	**wei-xian**	危险!

CUSTOMS AND ENTRY REQUIREMENTS

Travel to China is no longer the complicated procedure it was in the past. At first there were business visits by invitation only, then trips by groups on rigidly controlled tours, then more flexible package tours and, finally, independent individual travel. The regulations change more quickly than books can be updated. For the latest information, be sure to consult a qualified travel agent or Chinese consulate.

Visas

Every visitor to China must possess a valid passport and a visa issued by the Chinese authorities. Tour groups might be issued group visas, a single document listing the particulars of all the participants. The paperwork in this case is handled by the travel agency. Be sure to determine your need for a visa well in advance of your departure.

Though the Chinese authorities say visas can be obtained on arrival at major Chinese airports, independent travellers would do well to apply in advance through the China International Travel Service (CITS), China Travel Service (CTS) or the nearest Chinese consulate or embassy. Travel agencies responsible for making reservations normally expedite the issuing of the documents. Additional charges are levied for individual visas, as well as for urgent service, if required. The minimum time for delivery varies from one day in Hong Kong to ten days in most other places.

Health Requirements

No special inoculation certificates are required, except for visitors arriving in China within six days of leaving or passing through an area infected by yellow fever. Precautions against malaria are recommended for travellers planning to visit certain low-lying rural areas. It's wise to consult your doctor or appropriate health agency before departure for updates.

Customs Regulations

Before arrival you will have filled in a customs declaration form listing any watches, jewellery, cameras or electronic devices in your possession. When you leave China at the end of your trip, you might be asked to prove that you are taking with you all the items on the list, except for goods declared as gifts.

In general, it is forbidden to carry into China the following: arms and explosives, radio-transmitting equipment, fresh produce, live animals, material deemed subversive or pornographic and narcotics. The duty-free allowance for tourists entering China consists of two bottles of alcoholic beverages (not exceeding 2 litres total); 400 cigarettes; food, clothing and medicine for personal use; and any quantity of foreign currency. You should declare sums of cash exceeding US$5,000.

Leaving China

Foreign travellers are generally paid little attention, especially as they arrive in increasing numbers in China. The officer on duty might ask you to produce any or all items listed on your customs declaration form (cameras, watches and so forth). Keep receipts of purchases made in China in case any questions arise. Note that antiques may not be exported from China unless a special wax seal is attached (and antiques dating from before 1796 may not be exported at all).

To change money on departure, you might need to show your exchange receipts.

E

ELECTRICITY

In principle the electricity supply everywhere in China is 220 volts/50 cycles. In practice the voltage lapses significantly from time to time. Socket types and sizes vary, but hotels can usually lend adapters.

EMBASSIES IN BEIJING

Australia: 21 Dongzhimenwai Dajie, Beijing, tel: (10) 5140-4111; fax: (10) 5140-4292; <www.austemb.org.cn>

Canada: 19 Dongzhimenwai Dajie, Beijing, tel: (10) 6532-3536; fax: (10) 6532-5544; <www.canada.org.cn>

France: 3 Dongsan Jie, Sanlitun, Beijing, tel: (10) 8532-8080; fax: (10) 8532-4841; <www.consulfrance-pekin.org>

Germany: 17 Dongzhimenwai Dajie, Beijing, tel: (10) 8329-000; fax: (10) 6532-5336; <www.deutschebotschaft-china.org>

Republic of Ireland: 3 Ritan Donglu, Beijing, tel: (10) 6532-2691; fax: (10) 6532-6857; <www.ireland-china.com.cn>

Italy: 2 Dong'er Jie, Sanlitun, Beijing, tel: (10) 6532-2131; fax: (10) 6532-4676

New Zealand: 1 Dong'er Jie, Ritan Lu, Beijing, tel: (10) 6532-2731; fax: (10) 6532-4317; <www.nzembassy.com>

United Kingdom: Kerry Centre, 11 Guanghua Lu, Beijing, tel: (10) 8529-6600; fax: (10) 8529-6081; <www.uk.cn>

USA: 3 Xiushui Beijie, Jianguomenwai Dajie, Beijing, tel: (10) 6532-3831; fax: (10) 6532-6057; <www.beijing.usembassy-china.org.cn>

EMERGENCIES

See Health and Medical Care and Police.

G

GETTING THERE

By Air

Many international airlines in North America, Europe, Asia and Oceania have direct or connecting fights to Beijing, Shanghai and Hong Kong. CAAC, the Civil Aviation Administration of China, consists of more than 20 small airlines; Air China, China Eastern and China Southern (the three largest) offer some international flights.

From Europe. Both Chinese and European airlines offer flights to Beijing or Shanghai from London, Frankfurt, Paris, Copenhagen, Bucharest, Brussels, Helsinki, Vienna, Madrid, Zurich and other gateways. The airlines of certain countries en route, such as India, Pakistan, Iran or Russia, advertise bargain fares.

From North America. Direct flights to Hong Kong, Beijing and Shanghai operate from the west coast, with convenient connections to many North American cities. Some airlines link North America to Beijing via Tokyo or Hong Kong. It is also possible to travel by way of Europe (which may be less expensive, to compensate for the longer journey). If time and money are of secondary importance, look into round-the-world fares; some airlines offer special tariffs and unlimited stopovers as incentives.

From Australia and New Zealand. There are regularly scheduled flights from Melbourne, Sydney and Auckland to both Beijing and Shanghai, including several nonstop flights each week from Sydney.

By Sea

Chinese ports are on the route of several luxury cruise ship lines as well as for various regional carriers. Among the favourite destinations are Hong Kong, Shanghai and Xingang (the new harbour of Tianjin, the port nearest to Beijing). Other tourist ports include Xiamen (Amoy), Qingdao, Dalian and Yantai. Cruise ship companies sometimes offer their passengers excursions by rail or air; you leave the ship in one city and pick it up a couple of days later at another, spending the intervening time sightseeing inland – at extra cost, of course.

Touring Options in China

Until relatively recently the options open to the traveller to China were fairly limited. Now hundreds of cities and scenic spots are open to foreign visitors. Itineraries are varied, and specialist tours provide interesting alternatives to the usual tourist routes. Independent travel has become common, if not always easy.

Group Travel

Many tour operators in Europe and the United States offer group tours to China. The cost usually includes flight, full-board accommodation in China, excursions, internal travel in China, services of local guides and interpreters, and often finishing with a couple of nights in Hong Kong at the end of the trip. Groups consist of between 12 and 50 people, and the tour follows a fixed itinerary that takes in three to six cities. The duration of the trip might be from eight days to three weeks. Visits to farms, factories, hospitals, schools and other places difficult to visit on one's own may be included on a group tour, as well as trips to the top historic and scenic locations. Evening entertainment might include ethnic dance and music or a Chinese opera. Be prepared, though, for last-minute changes in itinerary and pre-planned activities. Most tours cannot be sure of the exact agenda until arrival in China (and sometimes not even then).

Special Interest and Adventure Tours

Alternative itineraries (but still in group format) are available for travellers with specialist interests: from acupuncture to archaeology, martial arts to minority cultures. On these tours, time might be spent in meetings with professional counterparts or visiting relevant institutions or sites. For those with a yen for adventure, there are tours featuring trekking, mountain climbing, wilderness exploration and cross-country cycling.

Independent Travel

Those travelling independently will have more opportunity to wander off the beaten track, although making one's own travel arrangements in China can be daunting. Many independent travellers enter China from Hong Kong. Part of China since 1997 and known officially as the 'Hong Kong Special Administrative Region' (SAR), this is the easiest place to obtain last-minute visas and make travel arrangements. There are air, rail, road and sea links between Hong Kong and many major destinations in China.

Private travel agencies in Hong Kong offer a variety of all-inclusive China tours, from a one-day excursion across the border to a full two- or three-week agenda taking in major cities and sights. Independent travellers can also make arrangements in Hong Kong through the local offices of China Travel Service (CTS) or China International Travel Service (CITS). In general, CTS handles travel for Overseas Chinese, while CITS (Guoji Luxingshe) is responsible for foreign tourists, although this distinction is fading. Flights into China can also be booked using Hong Kong-based Dragonair.

Many travellers, especially setting off from Hong Kong, prefer to travel on their own but with hotel and transport reservations made in advance and the assistance of guides who meet them at each location. This form of independent travel can be set up overseas or in Hong Kong by private travel agencies specialising in China. CITS can set up these assisted itineraries even after your initial arrival in China. Just name your destination and travel requirements in detail, and their agents can make all the arrangements speedily, although often for a considerable fee.

GUIDES AND INTERPRETERS

Package-tour travellers are sometimes overwhelmed with guides: an escort from the travel agency, a Chinese 'national' guide, a co-ordinator attached to one of the major offices of CITS, and a 'local' guide who knows the sights of a particular city or region. Independent tourists are not obliged to use the services of a guide or interpreter, but they often do so when booking local sightseeing tours. A guide permits you to use your time efficiently, eliminating the problems of making reservations and booking local transport while providing answers to your questions.

H

HAIR STYLISTS AND BARBERS

Larger hotels usually have a hairdresser and a barber, and you can find numerous hairdressers on the streets who offer reasonable prices. Head and neck massages may be included. Tipping is not necessary.

HEALTH AND MEDICAL CARE

At the end of 2005, China was one of the countries suffering from serious bird flu outbreaks. At the time of publication the disease had not yet passed from animal to human, but scientists are worried there could be human victims and that the virus may mutate into a form which could pass from human to human. Apart from this, there are no special health concerns. But you should consult your doctor before your trip to anticipate potential problems. Take with you any essential medications, as it is difficult or impossible to find Western medications and treatments. To avoid problems at customs, make sure all medication is clearly marked and in the original prescription bottle. If you plan to visit one of the regions in which malaria occurs, you must begin treatment before your trip and continue for a specified time after leaving the affected area.

The minor ailments that most often seem to strike foreign tourists are coughs, colds and sore throats. Digestive upsets occasionally result from drinking contaminated water or eating unhygienic food. You should avoid partially cooked or raw food, except the salad in top hotels.

Should you require medical care in China, your guide, hotel desk clerk or local CITS office will call a doctor or arrange for you to be taken to a hospital. Considering the language problem, it's a relief to have an interpreter when discussing symptoms and treatment. Most Chinese doctors, especially those treating foreign visitors, are extremely well qualified in Western medicine and can give expert care. (It is advised, however, that you carry your own sterile syringe in case an injection is required at a clinic or hospital.)

Treatment can involve both modern and traditional medicine if you request it. You can find clinics staffed by Western-trained doctors in cities with large expat populations, such as Beijing, Guangzhou, Shanghai, Tianjin and Qingdao. Treatment at these clinics is expensive, so taking out appropriate insurance is highly recommended.

HOLIDAYS

Offices and factories close nationwide on only four public holidays:

New Year's Day	1 January
Spring Festival (Chinese New Year)	January or February
Labour Day	1 May
National Day	1 October

The Spring Festival, determined by the lunar calendar, lasts for three days and is primarily a family holiday, while the holidays beginning 1 May and 1 October are both a week long. Other holidays, of modern origin, have little effect on daily life:

Women's Day	8 March
Youth Day	4 May
Children's Day	1 June

Communist Party Founding Day	1 July
Army Day	1 August

L

LANGUAGE

Chinese is the native tongue of more people than any other language. Yet communication among the Chinese themselves can be difficult. The written language that binds them is universal, but spoken Chinese is fragmented into dialects, some of them mutually incomprehensible. The vocabulary and grammar are the same, the writing is the same, but the pronunciation differs so much that a native of Guangzhou, for instance, cannot understand a citizen of Shanghai and vice versa. In the interests of national unity and understanding, the government vigorously encourages the use of *Putonghua*, a national language (known abroad as Mandarin Chinese) based on the dialect spoken in Beijing. But regional traditions are hard to demolish, even for a worthwhile cause.

0	ling	零	20	er-shi	二十
1	yi	一	21	er-shi-yi	二十一
2	er	二	22	er-shi-er	二十二
3	san	三	30	san-shi	三十
4	si	四	40	si-shi	四十
5	wu	五	50	wu-shi	五十
6	liu	六	60	liu-shi	六十
7	qi	七	70	qi-shi	七十
8	ba	八	80	ba-shi	八十
9	jiu	九	90	jiu-shi	九十
10	shi	十	100	yi-bai	一百
11	shi-yi	十一	101	yi-bai ling-yi	一百零一
12	shi-er	十二	200	er-bai	二百
13	shi-san	十三	1000	yiqian	一千

Putonghua is composed less of vowels and consonants than of syllables, consisting of a consonant of homonyms (words of different meaning but with identical spelling). In reality every syllable is pronounced with one of four tones (high, rising, falling-rising and falling). An example of how tones affect meaning: *ma* pronounced with a high tone means 'mother', with a rising tone 'hemp', with a falling-rising tone 'horse', and with a falling tone 'to curse' or 'to shout at'. It is very difficult for non-natives even to hear these tones, let alone reproduce them – hence the phonetic transliteration system used here has been simplified, and excludes tonal markers.

Written Chinese – the pictographs that have told the story of China for thousands of years – has no relation to the sound of the spoken language. In the interests of greater literacy, the government has simplified many of the traditional characters, but not enough to make it easy for foreigners. They have also inaugurated a new universal system for romanising Chinese words: the *pinyin* (literally 'phonetic sound') system is the reason 'Peking' is now written 'Beijing'.

Pronouncing *pinyin* has its own nuances and complications. Among the biggest stumbling blocks are the following consonants (accompanied by approximate English equivalents).

c	like ts in the word 'i**ts**'
g	hard g as in 'give'
h	like ch in Scottish 'lo**ch**'
j	like j in 'jeer'
q	similar to ch in '**ch**eer'
x	like sh in '**sh**ip'
z	like ds in 'ki**ds**'
zh	like j in 'jug'

The great majority of Chinese people know only a few standard phrases of English, and conversations can become painfully stilted. Hotel and airline employees and others who deal with foreigners have usually learned enough English to cope with everyday problems. Tour guides are trained to specialise in one or more foreign languages, but not all of them have a firm grasp of English. To make yourself understood, you might need to speak slowly, clearly and simply.

LAUNDRY AND DRY CLEANING

Hotels process laundry and dry cleaning quickly and efficiently; same-day or express service is common. Laundry bags and price lists are provided in your room. Ironing is also available in many hotels. There are laundries and dry cleaners *(ganxi)* outside hotels, but they are inconvenient for most foreigners to use. Launderettes (self-service laundries) are virtually nonexistent.

LOST PROPERTY

In China the property of foreigners is so conspicuous that it doesn't usually stay lost for long. The Beijing Public Security Bureau has often returned to foreign visitors and residents their cameras, luggage and even considerable quantities of cash. If you lose something, start the search by informing your guide or hotel desk.

M

MAPS

Hotels and tourist offices often issue free English-language tourist maps of major cities such as Beijing, Shanghai and Guangzhou. Maps can also be bought from hawkers outside railway stations, at bookshops, newspaper kiosks and tourist sights, although most maps are available in Chinese only. Transport maps are useful for bus routes, but many of these are in Chinese only.

MEDIA

Newspapers and Magazines

Some foreign publications are sold at the news kiosks of major hotels, most commonly the *International Herald Tribune*, the *Asian Wall Street Journal*, the *South China Morning Post* (from Hong Kong) and the *USA Today International Edition*. International weekly news magazines such as *Newsweek*, and even some fashion and sports magazines are sometimes available, although in smaller or more remote places you might find nothing in a foreign language at any newsstand.

The Chinese English-language newspaper, *China Daily*, and its weekly publications, *Beijing Weekend* and *Shanghai Star*, can be found at hotels and newsstands in most cities, although with considerable delays in outlying regions. These cover Chinese and foreign news plus tourist features, sports and even stock market reports.

Beijing, Guangzhou, Shanghai, Tianjin and Qingdao have some good magazines aimed at ex-pats, which are a useful source of local information and events listings. Such official government periodicals as *Beijing Review* and *China Pictorial* are widely available in many languages.

Television and Radio

Whether or not you understand Chinese, you will probably have a chance to catch a glimpse of the state-run television system. Features include the Chinese equivalent of soap operas, news bulletins, Chinese operas, films, sports events and relentless advertising. Virtually all hotel rooms come with TVs (usually with CCTV9, the English-language channel), while many hotels also offer closed-circuit broadcasts of foreign-language films and satellite TV.

Some English-language programmes of interest to tourists, including news and weather reports, are broadcast on Chinese radio. In most parts of the country, a short-wave transistor can pick up the BBC World Service, Voice of America and Radio Australia.

MONEY

Currency. The standard currency in China, called *renminbi* ('people's money', abbreviated as RMB), is based on the *yuan* (colloquially *kuai*), which is divided into 100 *fen*. Ten *fen* make a *jiao* (colloquially *mao*). For the most part, you will be using *yuan* notes, which come in denominations of 1, 2, 5, 10, 20, 50 and 100.

Banks and currency exchange. Foreign currency and travellers cheques can be exchanged for RMB in hotels, at special counters in the Bank of China and at Friendship Stores (see OPENING HOURS). You'll have to show your passport. Keep your receipt, in case you want to convert excess Chinese money to foreign currency when leaving the country (your only chance, as RMB is not currently convertible outside of China). There is some black-market currency exchange activity, but the exchange rates offered are barely better than the official rate, and it's not worth running the risk of being short-changed, receiving counterfeit bills, or being arrested.

Credit cards and travellers cheques. Credit cards are accepted more and more in tourist areas; look for the familiar emblems in hotels, some restaurants, and Friendship Stores. ATM machines with international access have appeared in large cities, making cash withdrawals possible, but don't count on finding such machines in many places. Certain branches of the Bank of China and some hotels can also make cash advances on your credit card, and most major hotels accept credit cards to pay all bills. Travellers cheques are recognised at money-exchange counters in hotels, banks and some shops. China is still largely a cash society, and most transactions outside the big hotels will require RMB. For example, most transport costs – domestic bus and train tickets – are paid in cash, although air tickets can often be bought with a credit card.

OPENING HOURS

Shops. Friendship Stores and department stores are usually open 9am–7pm (8pm in summer) seven days a week, including public holidays. Local shops sometimes stay open later.

Banks are generally open 8am to around 5pm Monday to Friday, with a lunch break from noon to 1.30pm. In large hotels, foreign-exchange facilities and desks are routinely open 24 hours, seven days a week, but be sure to enquire about exact hours when you check in.

Post office branches in hotels typically operate 8am–6pm Monday to Saturday, and 8am–noon Sunday.

Hairdressers and barbers stay open until at least 7pm, later in hotels.

Museum hours are generally 9am–4pm or later, six or seven days a week; if they close for one day, it is usually Monday. Temples are normally open 8am–5pm every day of the week.

Restaurants are typically open 8am–10am for breakfast, 11.30am–2pm for lunch, and 5pm–8.30pm for dinner, although these hours can vary considerably. In large towns and cities, for instance, restaurants tend to stay open later.

P

PHOTOGRAPHY

Although most modern department stores and a growing number of camera and film processing shops sell international brands of film, it's best to bring fresh rolls of your favourite film. With all the wonderful photo possibilities, you'll probably use more film than usual. One-hour or overnight film processing is available in main cities, but for absolute reliability most tourists still prefer to develop film at home. Bring a recharger for your digital camera or camcorder: you will be able to use it in your hotel, who can supply a plug adapter.

As a courtesy, always ask permission before taking close-ups of people in China. Don't pressurise anyone – even your tour guide – to pose for photos. But general scenes of people and places are perfectly fine. To preserve military secrecy, it is forbidden to take pictures of bridges, tunnels, airports and soldiers.

POLICE

Armed police wear green uniforms and peaked caps displaying the national insignia. Tourists commonly confuse the police with members of the air force, who wear an identical uniform except for the red star on the cap. The emergency telephone number for police assistance is 110.

R

RELIGION

Many houses of worship that were closed, damaged or destroyed during the Cultural Revolution have been restored to use. China has a sizeable Christian population and services are held at Roman Catholic and Protestant churches throughout China, even in small towns. If you wish to attend a religious service, give your guide advance warning so your request can be accommodated in the general schedule.

RESTAURANTS

Convenience and comfort might tempt you to eat all your meals in your hotels' dining rooms. After all, they are near at hand and predictable, with a menu in a more-or-less recognisable English; the waiters understand a foreigner's doubts and fears and might even lay out knives and forks for you. But even if the hotel food is good, you're missing the adventure of a real Chinese restaurant. Considering the importance the Chinese have always attached to eating well, you can expect plenty of choice and the possibility of great gourmet experiences.

As you travel through the country, look for restaurants specialising in regional dishes: Peking duck in Beijing, seafood in Shanghai and, if you're up to it, snake in Guangzhou. *(See Eating Out on page 218 for more detailed information.)* Your guide or hotel clerk can advise you in choosing a restaurant, ideally one rich in traditional atmosphere. If it's the high season, or if you are part of a large group, it's wise to have someone call ahead to reserve a table.

Watch out for restaurants that provide foreigners with an English menu displaying prices in excess of the Chinese version. Don't expect to be able to pay for meals by credit card. Tips are not expected in cheaper eateries, but a service charge will probably be levied in smarter establishments. Make sure that the restaurant is clean and that the food has been freshly prepared and is hot.

Bringing your own chopsticks is not considered an insult at all. Restaurants in China are often not heated, even in winter, so it is advisable to dress warmly.

When to eat. Hotels serve breakfast (Western-style as well as Chinese) 7am–8.30am or 9am, later in the far west to compensate for the delayed dawn. Breakfast is the only meal in hotels that normally offers a choice of Western-style or Chinese food. Lunch is served noon–2pm, and dinner is usually eaten 6pm–8pm or 8.30pm. Even banquets in China start early and finish by 9pm or 10pm. Some of the big hotels have restaurants that stay open after hours, for those who can't adapt to the Chinese timetable.

T

TIME ZONES

Although China extends across the longitudes, there is only one time zone in the whole country. This simplifies airline and broadcasting timetables, but in the far west it causes the sun to rise and set at peculiar hours in some seasons. China no longer changes the clocks for summer time. Standard time is GMT +8. The following chart shows time differences in winter:

Los Angeles	New York	London	**Beijing**	Sydney
4am	7am	noon	**8pm**	10pm

TIPPING

The Chinese authorities have traditionally discouraged the practice of tipping, and in general it is not necessary to tip, especially in top-class restaurants and hotels, where service charges are levied. A small gift – perhaps a souvenir of your home country – would be appropriate in certain cases (for a guide who has been extremely helpful, for instance). If the gift is refused, don't insist.

TOILETS

Public toilets throughout China, especially in towns and villages, are truly ghastly. Toilet facilities at tourist sights may be better, but prepare for overpowering smells and medieval standards of hygiene, and always carry a supply of tissues with you.

TOURIST INFORMATION

There is no nationwide chain of tourist offices in China, so travellers are left to rely on themselves, the regional tourist office (often badly run and inefficient), their hotel or a branch of China International Travel Service (CITS; known abroad as the China National Tourist Office, in China as *Guoji Luxingshe*), an operation that is far more travel agent than tourist office. CITS also has an English-language website <www.cnto.org> and overseas offices.

Beijing Tourist Information Centres: 27 Sanlitun Beilu; tel: 6417-6627; 10 Dengshikou Xijie; tel: 6512-3043

Branches of **China National Tourist Office** abroad include:

Australia: China National Tourist Office, 19th floor, 44 Market Street, Sydney NSW 2000; tel: (02) 9299 4057; fax: (02) 9290 1958.

Canada: China National Tourist Office, 480 University Avenue, Toronto, Ontario, M5G 1V2; tel: (416) 599-6636; fax: (416) 599-6382.

UK: China National Tourist Office, 4 Glentworth Street, London NW1 5PG; tel: (020) 7935 9787; fax: (020) 7487 5842.

USA: China National Tourist Office, 350 5th Avenue, Suite 6413, New York, NY 10118, tel (toll free): 1-888-760-8218; fax: (212) 760 8809.

TRANSPORT

Domestic Flights

Air service inside China is handled by several domestic airlines. In recent years, with the acquisition of new aircraft and the development of new airports, domestic air travel has become more comfortable. The air fleet is rapidly expanding and airports are being built and expanded throughout China, but delays are still common. On-board service on domestic flights varies greatly; refreshments might or might not be served, and souvenirs are often distributed.

Trains

The railway serves all the major cities and tourist centres. Although train trips can take a very long time, a journey on a Chinese train can be an enjoyable and enlightening experience.

Express trains cost more than regular service, and sleeping berths are extra. Seating is divided into the categories 'soft' and 'hard'. The latter is usually quite crowded. Loudspeakers frequently erupt in announcements or Chinese music, day and night. To reduce the volume, look for the knob under the table in private compartments.

Those travelling first class (both Chinese and foreigners) have access to a separate waiting room at provincial railway stations.

Boats

Travelling through China by boat has its delights: the scenery, the comfort and the relaxed pace. However, the number of boats and routes has dwindled in recent years as more people fly and travel by car and train. Ships link ports such as Shanghai, Tianjin, Dalian and Qingdao, although the schedules are sometimes inconvenient. Try to find time to take a river or lake ferryboat somewhere along the way to experience the crowds and the atmosphere.

Taxis

Almost everywhere in China, taxis are best ordered through the hotel. A full day's itinerary can be arranged in this way. Sometimes they can be hailed on the street; there are no taxi ranks. A restaurant or Friendship Store will call a taxi, but if you're out on your own sightseeing for a couple of hours, it might be more convenient to take a taxi and keep it waiting for you between stops. For short trips insist on using the meter *(dabiao)*; receipts are issued on demand.

Metro

China's first underground railway (subway), the Beijing Metro, carries over 70 million passengers a year quickly and cheaply. Except in rush hours, underground trains are far less crowded than local buses. There are also metro systems in Guangzhou, Shanghai, Shenzhen and Tianjin. Station signs are written in *pinyin* as well as Chinese characters.

W

WATER

Avoid tap water even in the large cities. You can safely drink the boiled water hotels provide in thermos flasks for making tea, and kettles are supplied in most four-star hotels. Bottled mineral water is available in restaurants.

WEIGHTS AND MEASURES

China uses the metric system, but traditional measurements endure in the marketplace. The Chinese market system is as follows:

Length		
1 *shichi*	33cm	1ft 1in
3 *shichi*	1 metre	3ft 3ins
1 *shili*	0.5km	0.31 mile (547yds)
2 *shili*	1km	0.62 mile (1,094yds)
Area		
1 *mu*	0.07 hectare	0.17 acre (837 sq yds)
15 *mu*	1 hectare	2.47 acres
Fluid measure		
1 *sheng*	1 litre	2.1 pints
Weight		
1 *jin*	0.5kg	1.1lb
2 *jin*	1 kg	2.2lb

INDEX